A Walker in the City

ALFRED STIEGLITZ: THE STEERAGE, 1907

Reproduced from *Camera Work*   Collection of The Museum of Modern Art

Also by Alfred Kazin

On Native Grounds
The Inmost Leaf
Contemporaries
Starting Out in the Thirties

EDITOR:

The Portable Blake
F. Scott Fitzgerald: The Man and His Work
The Stature of Theodore Dreiser
  (with Charles Shapiro)
Herman Melville, *Moby-Dick*
Emerson: A Modern Anthology
  (with Daniel Aaron)
The Works of Anne Frank
  (with Ann Birstein)
The Open Form: Essays for Our Time
Selected Short Stories of Nathaniel Hawthorne
Henry James, *The Ambassadors*
Walt Whitman, *Specimen Days*

ALFRED KAZIN

A WALKER
IN THE CITY

*The glories strung like beads on my smallest sights and hearings—
on the walk in the street, and the passage over the river.*
WHITMAN: Crossing Brooklyn Ferry

Drawings by Marvin Bileck

A Harvest/HBJ Book
Harcourt Brace Jovanovich
New York and London

HBJ

PRINTED IN THE UNITED STATES OF AMERICA

EFGH

Frontispiece photograph reproduced from *Camera Work*, collection of The Museum of Modern Art, New York.

FOR MICHAEL KAZIN

Excerpts from this book have appeared in Commentary *and* The New Yorker, *in somewhat different form, and are reprinted here by kind permission of the editors of these magazines.*

CHAPTERS OF THE JOURNEY

A Walker in the City

FROM THE SUBWAY

TO THE SYNAGOGUE

In every cry of every man,
In every infant's cry of fear,
In every voice, in every ban,
The mind-forg'd manacles I hear.

WILLIAM BLAKE: London

EVERY TIME I go back to Brownsville it is as if I had never been away. From the moment I step off the train at Rockaway Avenue and smell the leak out of the men's room, then the pickles from the stand just below the subway steps, an instant rage comes over me, mixed with dread and some unexpected tenderness. It is over ten years since I left to live in "the city"—everything just out of Brownsville was always "the city." Actually I did not go very far; it was enough that I could leave Brownsville. Yet as I walk those familiarly choked streets at dusk and see the old women sitting in front of the tenements, past and present become each other's faces; I am back where I began.

It is always the old women in their shapeless flowered housedresses and ritual wigs I see first; they give Brownsville back to me. In their soft dumpy bodies and the unbudging way they occupy the tenement stoops, their hands blankly folded in each other as if they had been sitting on these stoops from the beginning of time, I sense again the old foreboding that all my life would be like this. *Urime Yidn. Alfred, what do you want of us poor Jews?*

The early hopelessness burns at my face like fog the minute I get off the subway. I can smell it in the air as soon as I walk down Rockaway Avenue. It hangs over the Negro tenements in the shadows of the El-darkened street, the torn and flapping canvas sign still listing the boys who went to war, the stagnant wells of candy stores and pool parlors, the torches flaring at dusk over the vegetable stands and pushcarts, the neon-blazing fronts of liquor stores, the piles of *Halvah* and chocolate kisses in the windows of the candy stores next to the *News* and *Mirror*, the dusty old drugstores where urns of rose and pink and blue colored water still swing from chains, and where next door Mr. A.'s sign still tells anyone walking down Rockaway Avenue that he has pants to fit any color suit. It is in the faces of the kids, who before they are ten have learned that Brownsville is a nursery of tough guys, and walk with a springy caution, like boxers approaching the center of the ring. Even the Negroes who have moved into the earliest slums deserted by the Jews along Rock-away Avenue have been infected with the damp sadness of the place, and slouch along the railings of their wormy wooden houses like animals in a cage. The Jewish district drains out here, but eddies back again on the next street; *they* have no connection with it. A Gypsy who lives in one of the empty stores is being reproached by a tipsy Negro in a sweater and new pearl-gray fedora who has paid her to tell his fortune. *You promis' me, didnja? Didnja promis', you lousy f...?* His voice fills the street with the empty rattle of a wooden wheel turning over and over.

The smell of damp out of the rotten hallways accom-panies me all the way to Blake Avenue. Everything seems so small here now, old, mashed-in, more rundown even than I remember it, but with a heartbreaking familiarity at each door that makes me wonder if I can take in any-thing new, so strongly do I feel in Brownsville that I am walking in my sleep. I keep bumping awake at harsh in-tervals, then fall back into my trance again. In the last crazy afternoon light the neons over the delicatessens bathe all their wares in a cosmetic smile, but strip the street of every personal shadow and concealment. The torches over the pushcarts hold in a single breath of yellow flame the acid smell of half-sour pickles and herrings floating in their briny barrels. There is a dry rattle of loose newspa-per sheets around the cracked stretched skins of the "chiney" oranges. Through the kitchen windows along every ground floor I can already see the containers of milk, the fresh round poppy-seed evening rolls. Time for sup-per, time to go home. The sudden uprooting I always feel at dusk cries out in a crash of heavy wooden boxes; a dozen crates of old seltzer bottles come rattling up from the cellar on an iron roller. Seltzer is still the poor Jew's dinner wine, a mild luxury infinitely prized above the water out of the faucets; there can be few families in Brownsville that still do not take a case of it every week. It sparkles, it can be mixed with sweet jellies and syrups; besides, the water in Europe was often unclean.

In a laundry window off Dumont Avenue a printed poster with a Star of David at the head proclaims solidarity with "*our magnificent brothers in Palestine.*" A fiery breath of victory has come to Brownsville at last! Another poster calls for a demonstration against evictions. It is signed by one of those many subsidiaries of the Communist Party that I could detect if it were wrapped in twenty layers of disguise. "WORKERS AND PEOPLE OF BROWNSVILLE . . . !" Looking at that long-endured word *Landlord*, I feel myself quickening to the old battle cries.

And now I go over the whole route. Brownsville is that road which every other road in my life has had to cross.

When I was a child I thought we lived at the end of the world. It was the eternity of the subway ride into the city that first gave me this idea. It took a long time getting to "New York"; it seemed longer getting back. Even the I.R.T. got tired by the time it came to us, and ran up into the open for a breath of air before it got locked into its terminus at New Lots. As the train left the tunnel to rattle along the elevated tracks, I felt I was being jostled on a camel past the last way stations in the desert. Oh that ride from New York! Light came only at Sutter Avenue. First across the many stations of the Gentiles to the East River. Then clear across Brooklyn, almost to the brink of the ocean all our fathers crossed. All those first stations in Brooklyn—Clark, Borough Hall, Hoyt, Nevins, the junction of the East and West Side express lines—told me only that I was on the last leg home, though there was always a stirring of my heart at Hoyt, where the grimy subway platform was suddenly enlivened by Abraham and Straus's windows of ladies' wear. Atlantic Avenue was vaguely exciting, a crossroads, the Long Island railroad; I never saw a soul get in or out at Bergen Street; the Grand Army Plaza, with its great empty caverns smoky with dust and chewing-gum wrappers, meant Prospect Park and that stone path beside a meadow where as a child I ran off from my father one summer twilight just in time to see the lamplighter go up the path lighting from the end of his pole each gas mantle suddenly flaring within its corolla of pleated paper—then, that summer I first strayed off the block for myself, the steps leading up from the boathouse, the long stalks of grass wound between the steps thick with the dust and smell of summer—then, that great summer at sixteen, my discovery in the Brooklyn Museum of Albert Pinkham Ryder's cracked oily fishing boats drifting under the moon. Franklin Avenue was where the Jews began—but all middle-class Jews, *alrightniks*, making out "all right" in the New World, they were still Gentiles to me as they went out into the wide and tree-lined Eastern Parkway. For us the journey went on and on—past Nostrand, past Kingston, past Utica, and

only then out into the open at Sutter, overlooking Lincoln
Terrace Park, "Tickle-Her" Park, the zoo of our adoles-
cence, through which no girl could pass on a summer evening without its being understood forever after that she
was "in"; past the rickety "two-family" private houses
built in the fever of Brownsville's last real-estate boom;
and then into Brownsville itself—Saratoga, Rockaway,
and home. For those who lived still beyond, in East New
York, there was Junius, there was Pennsylvania, there was
Van Siclen, and so at last into New Lots, where the city
goes back to the marsh, and even the subway ends.

Yet it was not just the long pent-up subway ride that
led me to think of Brownsville as the margin of the city,
the last place, the car barns where they locked up the
subway and the trolley cars at night. There were always
raw patches of unused city land all around us filled with
"monument works" where they cut and stored tombstones,
as there were still on our street farmhouses and the remains of old cobbled driveways down which chickens
came squealing into our punchball games—but most of
it dead land, neither country nor city, with that look of
prairie waste I have so often seen on my walks along the
fringes of American cities near the freight yards. We were
nearer the ocean than the city, but our front on the ocean
was Canarsie—in those days the great refuse dump through
which I made my first and grimmest walks into the city
—a place so celebrated in New York vaudeville houses
for its squalor that the very sound of the word was always good for a laugh. CAN-NARR-SIE! They fell into the
aisles. But that was the way to the ocean we always took
summer evenings—through silent streets of old broken

houses whose smoky red Victorian fronts looked as if the paint had clotted like blood and had then been mixed with soot—past infinite weedy lots, the smell of freshly cut boards in the lumber yards, the junk yards, the marshland eating the pavement, the truck farms, the bungalows that had lost a window or a door as they tottered on their poles against the damp and the ocean winds. The place as I have it in my mind still reeks of the fires burning in the refuse dumps. Farms that had once been the outposts of settlers in Revolutionary days had crumbled and sunk like wet sand. Canarsie was where they opened the sluice gates to let the city's muck out into the ocean. But at the end was the roar of the Atlantic and the summer house where we stood outside watching through lattices the sports being served with great pitchers of beer foaming onto the red-checked tablecloths. Summer, my summer! Summer!

We were of the city, but somehow not in it. Whenever I went off on my favorite walk to Highland Park in the "American" district to the north, on the border of Queens, and climbed the hill to the old reservoir from which I could look straight across to the skyscrapers of Manhattan, I saw New York as a foreign city. There, brilliant and unreal, the city had its life, as Brownsville was ours. That the two were joined in me I never knew then —not even on those glorious summer nights of my last weeks in high school when, with what an ache, I would come back into Brownsville along Liberty Avenue, and, as soon as I could see blocks ahead of me the Labor Lyceum, the malted milk and Fatima signs over the candy stores, the old women in their housedresses sitting in front of the tenements like priestesses of an ancient cult, knew I was home.

We were the end of the line. We were the children of the immigrants who had camped at the city's back door, in New York's rawest, remotest, cheapest ghetto, enclosed on one side by the Canarsie flats and on the other by the hallowed middle-class districts that showed the way to New York. "New York" was what we put last on our address, but first in thinking of the others around us. *They* were New York, the Gentiles, America; we were Brownsville—*Brunzvil*, as the old folks said—the dust of the earth to all Jews with money, and notoriously a place that measured all success by our skill in getting away from it. So that when poor Jews left, *even* Negroes, as we said, found it easy to settle on the margins of Brownsville, and with the coming of spring, bands of Gypsies, who would rent empty stores, hang their rugs around them like a desert tent, and bring a dusty and faintly sinister air of carnival into our neighborhood.

They have built a housing project deep down the center of Brownsville, from Rockaway to Stone, cutting clean diagonal forms within the onlooking streets, and leaving at one end only the public school I attended as a boy. As I walked past those indistinguishable red prisms of city houses, I kept remembering what they had pulled down to make this *project*—and despite my pleasure in all this space and light in Brownsville, despite even my envious wonder what our own life would have been if *we* had lived, as soon all of New York's masses will live, just like

everybody else, still, I could not quite believe that what I
saw before me was real. Brownsville in that model quarter
looks like an old crone who has had a plastic operation,
and to my amazement I miss her old, sly, and withered
face. I miss all those ratty little wooden tenements, born
with the smell of damp in them, in which there grew up
how many schoolteachers, city accountants, rabbis, cancer specialists, functionaries of the revolution, and strong-
arm men for Murder, Inc.; I miss that affected squirt who
always wore a paste diamond on his left pinky and one
unforgotten day, taught me to say *children* for *kids;* I
miss the sinister "Coney Island" dives where before, during, and after the school day we all anxiously gobbled
down hot dogs soggy in sauerkraut and mustard, and I
slid along the sawdust floor fighting to get back the violin
the tough guys always stole from my locker for a joke; I
miss the poisonous sweetness I used to breathe in from the
caramels melting inside the paper cartons every time I
passed the candy wholesaler's on my way back from
school; I miss the liturgical refrain *Kosher-Bosher* lettered
on the windows of the butcher shops; the ducks at Thanks-
giving hanging down the doorways of the chicken store;
the clouds of white dust that rose up behind the windows
of the mattress factory. Above all I miss the fence to the
junk yard where I would wait with my store of little red
volumes, THE WORLD'S GREATEST SELECTED SHORT STORIES,
given us gratis by the *Literary Digest,* hoping for a glimpse
of a girl named Deborah. At eleven or twelve I was so
agonizedly in love with her, not least because she had
been named after a prophetess in Israel, that I would stand
at the fence for hours, even creep through the junk yard

to be near her windows, with those little red books always in my hand. At home I would recite to myself in triumph the great lines from Judges: *Desolate were the open towns in Israel, they were desolate, until that I arose, Deborah.* . . . . But near her I was afraid, and always took along volumes of THE WORLD'S GREATEST SELECTED SHORT STORIES as a gift, to ease my way into her house. She had five sisters, and every one of them always seemed to be home whenever I called. They would look up at me standing in their kitchen with the books in my hand, and laugh. "Look, boychik," the eldest once said to me in a kindly way, "you don't have to *buy* your way in here every time with those damned books just to see Deborah! Come on your own!"

There is something uncanny now about seeing the old vistas rear up at each end of that housing project. Despite those fresh diagonal walks, with their trees and children's sandboxes and Negro faces calmly at home with the white, so many of the old tenements have been left undisturbed on every side of the project, the streets beyond are so obviously just as they were when I grew up in them, that it is as if they had been ripped out of their original pattern and then pasted back again behind the unbelievable miniatures of the future.

To make that housing project they have torn away the lumber yard; the wholesale drygoods store where my dressmaker mother bought the first shirts I ever wore that she did not make herself; how many poolrooms; and that to me sinister shed that was so long a garage, but before that, in the days of the silents, a movie house where every week, while peddlers went up and down the aisles hawking ice-cream bricks and orange squeeze, I feasted in my terror and joy on the "episodes." It was there one afternoon, between the damp coldness in the movie house and the covetous cries of the peddlers, that I was first seized by that bitter guilt I always felt in the movies whenever there was still daylight outside. As I saw Monte Blue being locked into an Iron Maiden, it suddenly came on me that the penalty for my delicious reveries might be just such a death—a death as lonely, as sickeningly remote from all human aid, as the one I saw my hero calmly prepare to face against the yellow shadows of deepest Asia. Though that long-forgotten movie house now comes back on me as a primitive, folksy place—every time the main door was opened to let in peddlers with fresh goods, a hostile mocking wave of daylight fell against the screen, and in the lip-reading silence of the movies I could hear the steady whir and clacking of the machine and the screech of the trolley cars on Rockaway Avenue—I instantly saw in that ominous patch of light the torture box of life-in-death, some reproach calling out the punishment for my sin.

A sin, perhaps, only of my own devising; the sin I recorded against all idle enjoyment, looking on for its own sake alone; but a sin. The daylight was for grimness and labor.

I see that they have also torn out that little clapboard Protestant church that stood so long near the corner of Blake Avenue. It was the only church I ever saw in our neighborhood—the others were the Russian Orthodox meeting-house in East New York, and the Catholic church

on East New York Avenue that marked the boundary, as
I used to think of it, between us and the Italians stretch-
ing down Rockaway and Saratoga to Fulton. That little
clapboard church must have been the last of its kind sur-
viving from the days when all that land was owned by
Scottish farmers. I remember the hymns that rolled out of
the church on Sunday mornings, and how we sniffed as
we went by. All those earnest, faded-looking people in
their carefully brushed and strangely old-fashioned clothes
must have come down there from a long way off. I never
saw any of them except on Sunday mornings—the women
often surprisingly quite fat, if not so fat as ours, and looking rather timid in their severe dresses and great straw hats
with clusters of artificial flowers and wax berries along
the brim as they waited for each other on the steps after
the service; the men very stiff in their long four-buttoned
jackets. They did not belong with us at all; I could never
entirely believe that they were really there. One afternoon
on my way back from school my curiosity got the better
of me despite all my fear of Gentiles, and I stealthily crept
in, never having entered a church in my life before, to ex-
amine what I was sure would be an exotic and idolatrous
horror. It was the plainest thing I had ever seen—not, of
course, homey, lived-in, and smelling of sour wine, snuff,
and old prayer books, like our little wooden synagogue
on Chester Street, but so varnished-clean and empty and
austere, like our school auditorium, and so severely reserved above the altar and in the set rows of wooden
pews to the service of an enigmatic cult, that the chief
impression it made on me, who expected all Christians to
be as fantastic as albinos, was that these people were not,

apparently, so completely different from us as I had imagined. I was bewildered. What really held me there was the number of things written in English. I had associated God only with a foreign language. Suspended from the ceiling over the altar was a great gold-wood sign on which the black Gothic letters read: I AM THE RESURRECTION AND THE LIFE. I remember standing in the doorway, longing to go all the way up the aisle, then suddenly running away. The distance from that doorway to the altar was the longest gap in space I had ever seen.

All my early life lies open to my eye within five city blocks. When I passed the school, I went sick with all my old fear of it. With its standard New York public-school brown brick courtyard shut in on three sides of the square and the pretentious battlements overlooking that cockpit in which I can still smell the fiery sheen of the rubber ball, it looks like a factory over which has been imposed the façade of a castle. It gave me the shivers to stand up in that courtyard again; I felt as if I had been mustered back into the service of those Friday morning "tests" that were the terror of my childhood.

It was never learning I associated with that school: only the necessity to succeed, to get ahead of the others in the daily struggle to "make a good impression" on our teachers, who grimly, wearily, and often with ill-concealed distaste watched against our relapsing into the natural savagery they expected of Brownsville boys. The white, cool, thinly ruled record book sat over us from their desks all day long, and had remorselessly entered into it each day

—in blue ink if we had passed, in red ink if we had not—
our attendance, our conduct, our "effort," our merits and
demerits; and to the last possible decimal point in calcula-
tion, our standing in an unending series of "tests"—surprise
tests, daily tests, weekly tests, formal midterm tests, final
tests. They never stopped trying to dig out of us whatever
small morsel of fact we had managed to get down the
night before. We had to prove that we were really alert,
ready for anything, always in the race. That white thinly
ruled record book figured in my mind as the judgment
seat; the very thinness and remote blue lightness of its
lines instantly showed its cold authority over me; so much
space had been left on each page, columns and columns in
which to note down everything about us, implacably and
forever. As it lay there on a teacher's desk, I stared at it all
day long with such fear and anxious propriety that I had
no trouble believing that God, too, did nothing but keep
such record books, and that on the final day He would
face me with an account in Hebrew letters whose phonetic
dots and dashes looked strangely like decimal points count-
ing up my every sinful thought on earth.

All teachers were to be respected like gods, and God
Himself was the greatest of all school superintendents.
Long after I had ceased to believe that our teachers could
see with the back of their heads, it was still understood,
by me, that they knew everything. They were the dele-
gates of all visible and invisible power on earth—of the
mothers who waited on the stoops every day after three
for us to bring home tales of our daily triumphs; of the
glacially remote Anglo-Saxon principal, whose very name
was King; of the incalculably important Superintendent of

Schools who would someday rubberstamp his name to the bottom of our diplomas in grim acknowledgment that we had, at last, given satisfaction to him, to the Board of Superintendents, and to our benefactor the City of New York —and so up and up, to the government of the United States and to the great Lord Jehovah Himself. My belief in teachers' unlimited wisdom and power rested not so much on what I saw in them—how impatient most of them looked, how wary—but on our abysmal humility, at least in those of us who were "good" boys, who proved by our ready compliance and "manners" that we wanted to get on. The road to a professional future would be shown us only as we pleased *them*. *Make a good impression the first day of the term, and they'll help you out. Make a bad impression, and you might as well cut your throat.* This was the first article of school folklore, whispered around the classroom the opening day of each term. You made the "good impression" by sitting firmly at your wooden desk, hands clasped; by silence for the greatest part of the live-long day; by standing up obsequiously when it was so expected of you; by sitting down noiselessly when you had answered a question; by "speaking nicely," which meant reproducing their painfully exact enunciation; by "showing manners," or an ecstatic submissiveness in all things; by outrageous flattery; by bringing little gifts at Christmas, on their birthdays, and at the end of the term—the well-known significance of these gifts being that they came not from us, but from our parents, whose eagerness in this matter showed a high level of social consideration, and thus raised our standing in turn.

It was not just our quickness and memory that were always being tested. Above all, in that word I could never hear without automatically seeing it raised before me in gold-plated letters, it was our *character*. I always felt anxious when I heard the word pronounced. Satisfactory as my "character" was, on the whole, except when I stayed too long in the playground reading; outrageously satisfactory, as I can see now, the very sound of the word as our teachers coldly gave it out from the end of their teeth, with a solemn weight on each dark syllable, immediately struck my heart cold with fear—they could not believe I really had it. Character was never something you had; it had to be trained in you, like a technique. I was never very clear about it. On our side *character* meant demonstrative obedience; but teachers already had it—how else could they have become teachers? They had it; the aloof Anglo-Saxon principal whom we remotely saw only on ceremonial occasions in the assembly was positively encased in it; it glittered off his bald head in spokes of triumphant light; the President of the United States had the greatest conceivable amount of it. Character belonged to great adults. Yet we were constantly being driven onto it; it was the great threshold we had to cross. *Alfred Kazin, having shown proficiency in his course of studies and having displayed satisfactory marks of character* . . . Thus someday the hallowed diploma, passport to my further advancement in high school. But there—I could already feel it in my bones —they would put me through even more doubting tests of character; and after that, if I should be good enough and bright enough, there would be still more. *Character* was a bitter thing, racked with my endless striving to please. The school—from every last stone in the courtyard to the battlements frowning down at me from the walls—was only the stage for a trial. I felt that the very atmosphere of learning that surrounded us was fake—that every lesson, every book, every approving smile was only a pretext for the constant probing and watching of me, that there was not a secret in me that would not be decimally measured into that white record book. All week long I lived for the blessed sound of the dismissal gong at three o'clock on Friday afternoon.

I was awed by this system, I believed in it, I respected its force. The alternative was "going bad." The school was notoriously the toughest in our tough neighborhood, and the dangers of "going bad" were constantly impressed upon me at home and in school in dark whispers of the "reform school" and in examples of boys who had been picked up for petty thievery, rape, or flinging a heavy inkwell straight into a teacher's face. Behind any failure in school yawned the great abyss of a criminal career. Every refractory attitude doomed you with the sound "Sing Sing." Anything less than absolute perfection in school always suggested to my mind that I might fall out of the daily race, be kept back in the working class forever, or—dared I think of it? —fall into the criminal class itself.

I worked on a hairline between triumph and catastrophe. Why the odds should always have felt so narrow I understood only when I realized how little my parents thought of their own lives. It was not for myself alone that I was expected to shine, but for them—to redeem the constant anxiety of their existence. I was the first American child,

their offering to the strange new God; I was to be the
monument of their liberation from the shame of being—
what they were. And that there was shame in this was a
fact that everyone seemed to believe as a matter of course.
It was in the gleeful discounting of themselves—what do we
know?—with which our parents greeted every fresh victory in our savage competition for "high averages," for
prizes, for a few condescending words of official praise
from the principal at assembly. It was in the sickening invocation of "Americanism"—the word itself accusing us
of everything we apparently were not. Our families and
teachers seemed tacitly agreed that we were somehow to
be a little ashamed of what we were. Yet it was always
hard to say why this should be so. It was certainly not—
in Brownsville!—because we were Jews, or simply because
we spoke another language at home, or were absent on our
holy days. It was rather that a "refined," "correct," "nice"
English was required of us at school that we did not naturally speak, and that our teachers could never be quite sure
we would keep. This English was peculiarly the ladder of
advancement. Every future young lawyer was known by
it. Even the Communists and Socialists on Pitkin Avenue
spoke it. It was bright and clean and polished. We were expected to show it off like a new pair of shoes. When the
teacher sharply called a question out, then your name, you
were expected to leap up, face the class, and eject those
new words fluently off the tongue.

There was my secret ordeal: I could never say anything
except in the most roundabout way; I was a stammerer.
Although I knew all those new words from my private
reading—I read walking in the street, to and from the Chil-

dren's Library on Stone Avenue; on the fire escape and the roof; at every meal when they would let me; read even when I dressed in the morning, propping my book up against the drawers of the bureau as I pulled on my long black stockings—I could never seem to get the easiest words out with the right dispatch, and would often miserably signal from my desk that I did not know the answer rather than get up to stumble and fall and crash on every word. If, angry at always being put down as lazy or stupid, I did get up to speak, the black wooden floor would roll away under my feet, the teacher would frown at me in amazement, and in unbearable loneliness I would hear behind me the groans and laughter: *tuh-tuh-tuh-tuh.*

The word was my agony. The word that for others was so effortless and so neutral, so unburdened, so simple, so exact, I had first to meditate in advance, to see if I could make it, like a plumber fitting together odd lengths and shapes of pipe. I was always preparing words I could speak, storing them away, choosing between them. And often, when the word did come from my mouth in its great and terrible birth, quailing and bleeding as if forced through a thornbush, I would not be able to look the others in the face, and would walk out in the silence, the infinitely echoing silence behind my back, to say it all cleanly back to myself as I walked in the streets. Only when I was alone in the open air, pacing the roof with pebbles in my mouth, as I had read Demosthenes had done to cure himself of stammering; or in the street, where all words seemed to flow from the length of my stride and the color of the houses as I remembered the perfect tranquillity of a phrase in Beethoven's *Romance in F* I could sing back to myself as I walked—only then was it possible for me to speak without the infinite premeditations and strangled silences I toiled through whenever I got up at school to respond with the expected, the exact answer.

It troubled me that I could speak in the fullness of my own voice only when I was alone on the streets, walking about. There was something unnatural about it; unbearably isolated. I was not like the others! I was not like the others! At midday, every freshly shocking Monday noon, they sent me away to a speech clinic in a school in East New York, where I sat in a circle of lispers and cleft palates and foreign accents holding a mirror before my lips and rolling difficult sounds over and over. To be sent there in the full light of the opening week, when everyone else was at school or going about his business, made me feel as if I had been expelled from the great normal body of humanity. I would gobble down my lunch on my way to the speech clinic and rush back to the school in time to make up for the classes I had lost. One day, one unforgettable dread day, I stopped to catch my breath on a corner of Sutter Avenue, near the wholesale fruit markets, where an old drugstore rose up over a great flight of steps. In the window were dusty urns of colored water floating off iron chains; cardboard placards advertising hairnets, Ex-Lax; a great illustrated medical chart headed The Human Factory, which showed the exact course a mouthful of food follows as it falls from chamber to chamber of the body. I hadn't meant to stop there at all, only to catch my breath; but I so hated the speech clinic that I thought I would delay my arrival for a few minutes by eating my lunch on the steps. When I took the sandwich out of my bag, two

bitterly hard pieces of hard salami slipped out of my hand
and fell through a grate onto a hill of dust below the steps.
I remember how sickeningly vivid an odd thread of hair
looked on the salami, as if my lunch were turning stiff with
death. The factory whistles called their short, sharp blasts
stark through the middle of noon, beating at me where I
sat outside the city's magnetic circle. I had never known,
I knew instantly I would never in my heart again submit
to, such wild passive despair as I felt at that moment, sitting on the steps before THE HUMAN FACTORY, where little
robots gathered and shoveled the food from chamber to
chamber of the body. They had put me out into the streets,
I thought to myself; with their mirrors and their everlast-
ing pulling at me to imitate their effortless bright speech
and their stupefaction that a boy could stammer and stumble on every other English word he carried in his head,
they had put me out into the streets, had left me high and
dry on the steps of that drugstore staring at the remains of
my lunch turning black and grimy in the dust.

In the great cool assembly hall, dominated by the gold
sign above the stage KNOWLEDGE IS POWER, the windowsills
were lined with Dutch bulbs, each wedged into a mound
of pebbles massed in a stone dish. Above them hung a giant
photograph of Theodore Roosevelt. Whenever I walked
in to see the empty assembly hall for myself, the shiny
waxed floor of the stage dangled in the middle of the air
like a crescent. On one side was a great silk American flag,
the staff crowned by a gilt eagle. Across the dry rattling
of varnish-smelling empty seats bowing to the American

flag, I saw in the play of the sun on those pebbles wildly
sudden images of peace. *There* was the other land, crowned
by the severe and questioning face of Theodore Roosevelt,
his eyes above the curiously endearing straw-dry mustache, behind the pince-nez glittering with light, staring
and staring me through as if he were uncertain whether he
fully approved of me.

The light pouring through window after window in that
great empty varnished assembly hall seemed to me the most
wonderful thing I had ever seen. It was that thorough varnished cleanness that was of the new land, that light dancing off the glasses of Theodore Roosevelt, those green and
white roots of the still raw onion-brown bulbs delicately
flaring up from the hill of pebbles into which they were
wedged. The pebbles moved me in themselves, there were
so many of them. They rose up around the bulbs in delicately strong masses of colored stone, and as the sun fell
between them, each pebble shone in its own light. Looking
across the great rows of empty seats to those pebbles lining
the windowsills, I could still smell summer from some long
veranda surrounded by trees. On that veranda sat the
family and friends of Theodore Roosevelt. I knew the
name: Oyster Bay. Because of that picture, I had read *The
Boy's Life of Theodore Roosevelt;* knew he had walked
New York streets night after night as Police Commissioner,
unafraid of the Tenderloin gangsters; had looked into
Theodore Roosevelt's Letters to His Children, pretending
that those hilarious drawings on almost every page were
for me. *There* was America, I thought, the real America,
his America, where from behind the glass on the wall of

our assembly hall he watched over us to make sure we did right, thought right, lived right.

"Up, boys! Up San Juan Hill!" I still hear our roguish old civics teacher, a little white-haired Irishman who was supposed to have been with Teddy in Cuba, driving us through our Friday morning tests with these shouts and cries. He called them "Army Navy" tests, to make us feel big, and dividing the class between Army and Navy, got us to compete with each other for a coveted blue star. Civics was city government, state government, federal government; each government had functions; you had to get them out fast in order to win for the Army or the Navy. Sometimes this required filling in three or four words, line by line, down one side of the grimly official yellow foolscap that was brought out for tests. (In the tense silence just before the test began, he looked at us sharply, the watch in his hand ticking as violently as the sound of my heart, and on command, fifty boys simultaneously folded their yellow test paper and evened the fold with their thumbnails in a single dry sigh down the middle of the paper.) At other times it meant true-or-false tests; then he stood behind us to make sure we did not signal the right answers to each other in the usual way—for true, nodding your head; for false, holding your nose. You could hear his voice barking from the rear. *"Come on now, you Army boys! On your toes like West Point cadets! All ready now? Get set! Go! Three powers of the legislative branch? The judiciary? The executive? The subject of the fifteenth amendment? The capital of Wyoming? Come on, Navy! Shoot those landlubbers down! Give 'em a blast from your big guns right through the middle! The third article of the*

Bill of Rights? The thirteenth amendment? The sixteenth? True or false, Philadelphia is the capital of Pennsylvania. Up and at 'em, Navy! Mow them down! COME ON!!!" Our "average" was calculated each week, and the boys who scored 90 per cent or over were rewarded by seeing *their own names* lettered on the great blue chart over the blackboard. Each time I entered that room for a test, I looked for my name on the blue chart as if the sight of it would decide my happiness for all time.

Down we go, down the school corridors of the past smelling of chalk, lysol out of the open toilets, and girl sweat. The staircases were a gray stone I saw nowhere else in the school, and they were shut in on both sides by some thick unreflecting glass on which were pasted travel posters inviting us to spend the summer in the Black Forest. Those staircases created a spell in me that I had found my way to some distant, cool, neutral passageway deep in the body of the school. There, enclosed within the thick, green boughs of a classic summer in Germany, I could still smell the tense probing chalk smells from every classroom, the tickling high surgical odor of lysol from the open toilets, could still hear that continuous babble, babble of water dripping into the bowls. Sex was instantly connected in my mind with the cruel openness of those toilets, and in the never-ending sound of the bowls being flushed I could detect, as I did in the maddeningly elusive fragrance of cologne brought into the classroom by Mrs. B., the imminence of something severe, frightening, obscene. Sex, as they said in the "Coney Island" dives outside the school, was like going to the toilet; there was a great contempt in this that made me think of the wet rings left by our sneakers as we ran down the gray stone steps after school.

Outside the women teachers' washroom on the third floor, the tough guys would wait for the possible appearance of Mrs. B., whose large goiterous eyes seemed to bulge wearily with mischief, who always looked tired and cynical, and who wore thin chiffon dresses that affected us much more than she seemed to realize. Mrs. B. often went about the corridors in the company of a trim little teacher of mathematics who was a head shorter than she and had a mustache. Her chiffon dresses billowed around him like a sail; she seemed to have him in tow. It was understood by us as a matter of course that she wore those dresses to inflame us; that she *was* tired and cynical, from much practice in obscene lovemaking; that she was a "bad one" like the young Polish blondes from East New York I occasionally saw in the "Coney Island" dives sitting on someone's lap and smoking a cigarette. How wonderful and unbelievable it was to find this in a teacher; to realize that the two of them, after we had left the school, probably met to rub up against each other in the faculty toilet. Sex was a grim test where sooner or later you would have to prove yourself doing things to women. In the smell of chalk and sweat and the unending smirky babble of the water as it came to me on the staircase through my summer's dream of old Germany, I could feel myself being called to still another duty—to conquer Mrs. B., to rise to the challenge she had whispered to us in her slyness. I had seen pictures of it on the block—they were always passing them around between handball games—the man's face furious, ecstatic with lewdness as he proudly looked down at himself; the woman sniggering as she teased him with droplets from the contraceptive someone had just shown me in the gutter—its crushed, filmy slyness the very sign of the forbidden.

They had never said anything about this at home, and I thought I knew why. Sex was the opposite of books, of pictures, of music, of the open air, even of kindness. They would not let you have both. Something always lingered to the sound of those toilets to test you. In and out of the classroom they were always testing you. *Come on, Army! Come on, Navy!* As I stood up in that school courtyard and smelled again the familiar sweat, heard again the unending babble from the open toilets, I suddenly remembered how sure I had always been that even my failures in there would be entered in a white, thinly ruled, official record book.

On Belmont Avenue, Brownsville's great open street market, the pushcarts are still lined on each other for blocks, and the din is as deafening, marvelous, and appetizing as ever. They have tried to tone it down; the pushcarts are now confined to one side of the street. When I was a boy, they clogged both sides, reached halfway up the curb to the open stands of the stores; walking down the street was like being whirled around and around in a game of blind man's buff. But Belmont Avenue is still the merriest street in Brownsville. As soon as I walked into it from Rockaway, caught my first whiff of the herrings and pickles in their great black barrels, heard the familiarly

harsh, mocking cries and shouts from the market women—
*"Oh you darlings! Oh you sweet ones, oh you pretty ones!
Storm us! Tear us apart! Devour us!"*—I laughed right out
loud, it was so good to be back among *them*. Nowhere but
on Belmont Avenue did I ever see in Brownsville such open,
hearty people as those market women. Their shrewd open-
weather eyes missed nothing. The street was their native
element; they seemed to hold it together with their hands,
mouths, fists, and knees; they stood up in it behind their
stands all day long, and in every weather; they stood up
for themselves. In winter they would bundle themselves
into five or six sweaters, then putting long white aprons
over their overcoats, would warm themselves at fires lit
in black oil drums between the pushcarts, their figures
bulging as if to meet the rain and cold head-on in defiance.

I could hear them laughing and mock-crying all the way
to Stone Avenue, still imploring and pulling at every
woman on the street—*"Vayber! Vayber! Sheyne gute vayber! Oh you lovelies! Oh you good ones! Oh you pretty
ones! See how cheap and good! Just come over! Just taste!
Just a little look! What will it cost you to taste? How can
you walk on without looking? How can you resist us?
Oh! Oh! Come over! Come over! Devour us! Storm us!
Tear us apart! BARGAINS BARGAINS!!"* I especially
loved watching them at dusk, an hour before supper, when
the women would walk through to get the food at its
freshest. Then, in those late winter afternoons, when there
was that deep grayness on the streets and that spicy smell
from the open stands at dusk I was later to connect with
my first great walks inside the New York crowd at the
rush hour—then there would arise from behind the great

flaming oil drums and the pushcarts loaded with their separate mounds of shoelaces, corsets, pots and pans, stockings, kosher kitchen soap, memorial candles in their wax-
filled tumblers and glassware, "chiney" oranges, beet roots
and soup greens, that deep and good odor of lox, of salami,
of herrings and half-sour pickles, that told me I was truly
home.

As I went down Belmont Avenue, the copper-shining
herrings in the tall black barrels made me think of the ven-
eration of food in Brownsville families. I can still see the
kids pinned down to the tenement stoops, their feet help-
lessly kicking at the pots and pans lined up before them,
their mouths pressed open with a spoon while the great
meals are rammed down their throats. *"Eat! Eat! May you
be destroyed if you don't eat! What sin have I committed
that God should punish me with you! Eat! What will become of you if you don't eat! Imp of darkness, may you
sink ten fathoms into the earth if you don't eat! Eat!"*

We never had a chance to know what hunger meant.
At home we nibbled all day long as a matter of course.
On the block we gorged ourselves continually on "Nes-
sels," Hersheys, gumdrops, polly seeds, nuts, chocolate-
covered cherries, charlotte russe, and ice cream. A warm
and sticky ooze of chocolate ran through everything we
touched; the street always smelled faintly like the candy
wholesaler's windows on the way back from school. The
hunger for sweets, jellies, and soda water raged in us like
a disease; during the grimmest punchball game, in the middle of a fist fight, we would dash to the candy store to
get down two-cent blocks of chocolate and "small"—three-
cent—glasses of cherry soda; or calling "upstairs" from the

street, would have flung to us, or carefully hoisted down
at the end of a clothesline, thick slices of rye bread smeared
with chicken fat. No meal at home was complete without
cream soda, root beer, ginger ale, "celery tonic." We
poured jelly on bread; we poured it into the tea; we often
ate chocolate marshmallows before breakfast. At school
during the recess hour Syrian vendors who all looked alike
in their alpaca jackets and black velours hats came after us
with their white enameled trays, from which we took
Halvah, Turkish Delight, and three different kinds of
greasy nut-brown pastry sticks. From the Jewish vendors,
who went around the streets in every season wheeling their
little tin stoves, we bought roasted potatoes either in the
quarter or the half—the skins were hard as bark and still
smelled of the smoke pouring out of the stoves; apples
you ate off a stick that were encrusted with a thick glaze
of baked jelly you never entirely got down your throat
or off your fingers, so that you seemed to be with it all
day; *knishes;* paper spills of hot yellow chick peas. I
still hear those peddlers crying up and down the street—
"*Árbes! Árbes! Hayse gute árbes! Kinder! Kinder! Hayse
gute árbes!*" From the "big" Italians, whom we saw only
in summer, we bought watermelons as they drove their
great horse-smelling wagons down the street calling up to
every window—"Hey you ladies! *Hey ladies! Freschi* and
good!"—and from the "small" ones, who pushed carts
through the streets, paper cups of shaved ice sprinkled before our eyes with drops of lemon or orange or raspberry
syrup from a narrow water bottle.

But our greatest delight in all seasons was "delicatessen"
—hot spiced corned beef, pastrami, rolled beef, hard salami,

soft salami, chicken salami, bologna, frankfurter "specials" and the thinner, wrinkled hot dogs always taken with mustard and relish and sauerkraut, and whenever possible, to make the treat fully real, with potato salad, baked beans, and french fries which had been bubbling in the black wire fryer deep in the iron pot. At Saturday twilight, as soon as the delicatessen store reopened after the Sabbath rest, we raced into it panting for the hot dogs sizzling on the gas plate just inside the window. The look of that blackened empty gas plate had driven us wild all through the wearisome Sabbath day. And now, as the electric sign blazed up again, lighting up the words JEWISH NATIONAL DELICATESSEN, it was as if we had entered into our rightful heritage. Yet *Wurst* carried associations with the forbidden, the adulterated, the excessive; with spices that teased and maddened the senses to demand more, still more. This was food that only on Saturday nights could be eaten with a good conscience. Generally, we bought it on the sly; it was supposed to be bad for us; I thought it was made in dark cellars. Still, our parents could not have disapproved of it altogether. Each new mouthful of food we took in was an advantage stolen in the battle. The favorite injunction was to *fix yourself*, by which I understood we needed to do a repair job on ourselves. In the swelling and thickening of a boy's body was the poor family's earliest success. "Fix yourself!" a mother cried indignantly to the child on the stoop. "Fix yourself!" The word for a fat boy was *solid*.

   Pitkin Avenue weighs on me. As you go up from Belmont, the neon glare suddenly lights up all the self-conscious confusion of Brownsville's show street. Banks, Woolworth's, classy shops, loan companies, Loew's Pitkin, the Yiddish theater, the Little Oriental restaurant—except for Brownsville's ancestral stress in the food, the Yiddish theater, the left wing-right wing arguments around the tables in Hoffman's Cafeteria, the Zionist appeals along the route, it might be Main Street in any moderately large town. But as I walk it now, the people look strangely divided from each other as they pick, pick, pick at the lighted frippery in the windows, and I think of our one Emma Bovary, Mrs. E., whose wild longing for a nicer world than this led her to abandon her housework for half an hour every morning to sit *at a table* in the empty vegetarian restaurant; it made her feel so distinguished.

No other Brownsville street brings home to me so many of the external things I once lived with. Pitkin Avenue is what Brownsville is most proud of, for walking down it on a Saturday night, when all the lights are ablaze and the sharpies in their wide-brimmed Broadway hats waiting to pick up a girl outside the old United States Bank building look as if their greatest ambition were to be mistaken for prosperous Gentiles from Flatbush, a stranger might almost be persuaded that Brownsville is not, after all, so different. But it is the street I felt most alien to, and which I secretly hated. I can never forget the *surprise* I always felt walking into it a block from our house. After Pitkin Avenue, the tenement side streets always seemed especially dark.

On one side of Pitkin the landlords' protective association and the offices of the pious Tammany lawyers—the "leaders" of the community who could always sprinkle a few tearful words of Yiddish solidarity during the campaign and so deliver the vote to the organization. On the other, the gray marble savings bank in whose shadow the Communists and Socialists raged at each other alone under all their talk of France, Germany, Spain, India, China.

Standing there I seemed to see two long processions of militant ghosts passing down each side of me. Even as they flung at each other the old catchwords, accusations, battle cries, they were united in giving my despair of both a harsh, contemptuous and unbelieving look. How well I know that cult of all significance, those eyes trained with hopeful sharpness on every public event in the world, those palms wet with daily uncertainty of the future, the abstractions, the abstractions that filled every hour of talk about the *world situation* those nights you could hear evicted families weeping on the street. How all those ghosts still surround me as in my trance I walk Pitkin Avenue again. Where now is Mendy, with the venomous cowlick over his eyes, who went off from the slums of Thatford Avenue to disappear on the Ebro, in defense of "Spain," and before he left dismissed me forever in rage and contempt—"intellectuals are not even worth shooting"—because I doubted the omniscience of Josef Vissarionovitch Stalin? And David, my excellent if pedantical friend David, with those thick lenses before his eyes severe as Marxist method, who dutifully suppressed his love of chemistry and poetry to go down into the wilds of darkest Georgia to advance the cause of the Negro oppressed?

All bank corners on Pitkin Avenue were gathering places. Even banks that had failed in the depression and had closed their doors forever still kept their fascination for the groups that had always met outside them. Perhaps they hoped that by looking through the grilled windows long and intently enough they might see some of the money they had lost. In front of the old Municipal Bank on the corner of Stone—how my heart quickened as I went up to it—is a place where every Saturday morning about eleven my father and his fellow house painters gathered in one circle, carpenters and plasterers and bricklayers in theirs. The men came to talk shop, and if they were out of work, to get the nod from the union delegate or a boss, who walked about in the crowd calling hands to a new job. The men would stand around for hours—smoking, gossiping, boasting of their children, until it was time to go home for the great Sabbath midday meal. One of my greatest pleasures as a boy was to walk down Pitkin Avenue pretending I had no idea where my father was, and then to stand at his side listening to the racy, hard, pseudo-cynical painter talk. My father always introduced me around, very shyly but with unmistakable delight, as his *kaddish*. What an intense pride that word carried for him, and how it saddened me. *Kaddish* is the Hebrew prayer for the dead, read for a father by his son. Even among the hardened working-class skeptics—I never knew a painter who was devout; they all left that to their women—the term was kept up as a matter of course, out of fatherly pride: "See the one who comes after me!" But though I knew the word was only formally connected with death, I heard too much of death in our house, all through the year, to want to hear my father speak of it, even in jest; those meetings in front of the old Municipal Bank meant too much to me.

I liked listening to the painters talk about their famous

union boss, Jake the Bum, and to the unending disputes between left wing and right wing, which had been in friction with each other for so long, so automatically bristled and flared as soon as a word was said, that the embattled daily life of the union came alive for me. I liked especially hearing the men roll out those long curses against the "boss painters"—*may a black year befall them, the miserable bastards*—which made up, a little, for the insecurity of their trade. I was happy my father was a painter; I liked painters. They were not bent and cadaverous and pale, like my uncles and cousins in the garment lofts on Seventh Avenue; the smell of paint and plaster was still on their overcoats Saturday mornings; they had a kind of mock bravado that suited men who were always getting up on scaffolds and falling off scaffolds and rising off the ground with a curse to live another day; and who liked to think of themselves as great drinkers and boasters and lechers, knew how to laze on a job, how to drive an unpopular contractor crazy; thought of themselves all as great artists in their line; and never knew from one month to the next if they would be working, or where.

I can still hear my mother's anxious question each time my father returned from that labor pool in front of the Municipal Bank—*Geyst arbeten?* Will there be work this week? From the early 'thirties on, my father could never be sure in advance of a week's work. Even the "long" jobs never seemed to last very long, and if he was on an "outside" job, a rainy day was a day lost. It puzzled me greatly when I came to read in books that Jews are a shrewd people particularly given to commerce and banking, for all the Jews I knew had managed to be an exception to that rule. I grew up with the belief that the natural condition of a Jew was to be a propertyless worker like my painter father and my dressmaker mother and my dressmaker uncles and cousins in Brownsville—workers, kin to all the workers of the world, dependent entirely on the work of their hands. All happiness in our house was measured by the length of a job. The greatest imaginable bliss was a "busy season." It was unfortunate, but did not matter too much, if the boss was a bastard, a skinflint, a cheat, a no-good, so sharp with his men that one might—God forgive us—doubt that he was a Jew. All that was to be expected of him, was of his very essence as a boss—for a boss, as my mother once offhandedly defined the type in a sentence that lighted up for me our instinctive belief in the class struggle—a boss was a man who did nothing himself, sat by idly, enjoying himself, and got rich on the bitter toil of others. It was far more important to us that the boss be successful, full of work to give out. Let him be mean, let him be unspeakable, let him be hateful—he kept us alive. I remember it was said of a young painter cousin of mine, who had somehow managed to work six months steady, that he lived on his boss, meaning that there was something suspect about him; it was as if he had morally deserted the working class by getting too close to the boss—for how else could he have managed that triumph?

Chester Street at last, and the way home.

On my right hand the "Stadium" movie house—the sanctuary every Saturday afternoon of my childhood, the great dark place of all my dream life. On my left the little

wooden synagogue where I learned my duties as a Jew
and at thirteen, having reached the moral estate of a man,
stood up at the high desk before the Ark (*Blessed be He,
Our Lord and Our Shield!*) and was confirmed in the faith
of my fathers.

Right hand and left hand: two doorways to the East.
But the first led to music I heard in the dark, to inward-
ness; the other to ambiguity. That poor worn synagogue
could never in my affections compete with that movie
house, whose very lounge looked and smelled to me like
an Oriental temple. It had Persian rugs, and was marvel-
ously half-lit at all hours of the day; there were great semi-
arcs of colored glass above the entrance to the toilets, and
out of the gents' came a vaguely foreign, deliciously sting-
ing deodorant that prepared me, on the very threshold of
the movie auditorium itself, for the magic within. There
was never anything with such expectancy to it as that twi-
lit lounge. I would even delay in it a little, to increase my
pleasure in what lay ahead; and often shut my eyes just as
I entered the auditorium, knowing that as soon as I opened
them again a better world would take me in.

In the wonderful darkness of the movies there was nothing to remind me of Brownsville—nothing but the sudden
alarm of a boy who, reminding himself at six o'clock that
it was really time to get home, would in his haste let himself out by the great metal fire door in front. Then the
gritty light on Bristol Street would break up the images
on the screen with a meanness that made me shudder.

I always feared that light for the same reason: it seemed
to mock imagination. I could never finally leave the movies,
while the light of Saturday afternoon still filled the streets,

without feeling the sadness that Spinoza describes as coming after lust, and would stare amazed, numb and depleted at the mica dots gleaming in the pavement and at the people still busily moving up and down Chester Street. There was something in the everyday look of the streets that reproached me; they seemed to know I had come back to them unwillingly. But deep inside the darkness of the movies everything that was good in life, everything that spoke straight to the imagination, began in some instant dark fusion between the organ music from the pit and the cycles of terror that started up again each Saturday afternoon in the "episodes." Walking home afterward, everything I felt came to me as the first ominously repeated notes of Schubert's *Unfinished* when the hero jumped from roof to roof just ahead of the crooks; the horn calls in Weber's overture to *Oberon* when Tarzan fell into the lion trap, his mouth opening in a silent scream I heard all along my spine; Sinding's *Rustle of Spring* when the sky darkened just before a storm—music that was as uncontainable as water or light or air, that shifted its course with each new breath it took, and showed me the rapids, the storms, the plunging mountain falls of consciousness itself. Where were those notes racing in me? Oh where were they racing? What had that music been preparing for me so deep in the bowels of the earth? Whenever that shadowy organist in the pit, whose face I could never see as he bent over the faintly lighted rows of keys, began one of those three pieces he played for "episodes," my throat would beat wildly in premonition, but I knew a secret happiness, as if my mind had at last been encouraged to seek its proper concerns.

Not so in the synagogue. It was dark enough, but without any illusion or indulgence for a boy; and it had a permanently stale smell of snuff, of vinegar, of beaten and scarred wood in the pews, of the *rebbitsin's* cooking from the kitchen next door, of the dusty velvet curtains over the Ark, of the gilt brocade in the prayer shawls, of ancient prayer books and commentaries which in their chipped black bindings and close black print on the yellowing paper looked as if they had come down to us from Moses and the Prophets, with the reverent kiss of each generation in the margins. The synagogue was old, very old; it must once have been a farmhouse; it was one of the oldest things in Brownsville and in the world; it was old in every inch of the rotting wooden porch, in the crevices deep in the doors over the Ark, in the little company of aged and bearded men smelling of snuff who were to be seen there every day at twilight, wrapped in their blackstriped prayer shawls, their eyes turned to Jerusalem, mumbling and singing in their threadbare voices—"*Blessed, praised, glorified, extolled and exalted shall be the Holy Name of the Supreme King of Kings! Blessed is He, for He is the First and the Last, and besides Him there is no God!*"

As it was for Abraham and Isaac, Jacob and Benjamin . . . Old as the synagogue was, old as it looked and smelled in its every worn and wooden corner, it seemed to me even older through its ties to that ancestral world I had never seen. Its very name, Dugschitz, was taken from the little Polish village my mother came from; everyone in the congregation was either a relative or an old neighbor—a *lantsman*. I belonged to that synagogue as a matter of course; I was my mother's son. My father, as an honest Social

Democrat and enlightened free thinker, was tolerant in these matters, and with good-humored indifference let my mother claim me among her "brethren." When he came around to the synagogue at all, it was to exchange greetings at the New Year, and to listen, as he said, to the cantor trying for the high notes; he liked singing.

There was another synagogue halfway down the block, much larger and no doubt more impressive in every way; I never set foot in it; it belonged to people from another province in Russia. The little wooden synagogue was "our" place. All good *Dugschitzer* were expected to show up in it at least once a year, had their sons confirmed in it as a matter of course, and would no doubt be buried from it when their time came. Members of the congregation referred to each other in a homely familiar way, using not the unreal second names so many Jews in Russia had been given for the Czar's census, but the first names in their familiar order —Dovid Yossel's or Khannah Sorke's; some were known simply by some distinguishing physical trait, the Rakhmiel lame in one foot. There were little twists and turns to the liturgy that were strictly "ours," a particularly nostalgic way of singing out the opening words of prayers that only *Dugschitzer* could possibly know. If the *blind* Rakhmiel— the Rakhmiel in the back bench who was so nearsighted that he might fairly be described as blind—skipped two lines in the prayer book, the sexton would clutch his hands in despair and call out mockingly, *"Beneshalélem; Bless the Lord!* Will you just listen to the way he *reads?"* There were scornful little references to the way *outsiders* did things—people from Warsaw, for example, who gave every sound a pedantic roll; or Galicians, who, as everyone knew,

were coarse-grained, had no taste, took cream with her-
ring, and pronounced certain words in so uncouth a manner that it made you ache with laughter just to hear them.
What did it matter that our congregation was poor, our
synagogue small and drab? It was sufficient to the handful
of *us* in Brownsville, and from birth to death would re-
gather us in our ties to God, to the tradition of Israel, and
to each other. On a Saturday when a boy had been confirmed, and the last loving proud *Amen!* had been heard
from the women where they sat at the back separated from
us by a gauze curtain, and a table in an open space between the pews had been laden with nut-cake, fruit, her-
ring, and wine, and the brethren had gathered to toast the
boy and his parents and each other in their rejoicing for
Israel, we were all—no matter what we knew of each other
or had suffered from each other—one plighted family.

Though there was little in the ritual that was ever ex-
plained to me, and even less in the atmosphere of the synagogue that in my heart I really liked, I assumed that my
feelings in the matter were of no importance; I belonged
there before the Ark, with the men, sitting next to an
uncle. I felt a loveless intimacy with the place. It was not
exclusively a house of "worship," not frigid and formal as
we knew all churches were. It had been prayed in and
walked through and lived in with such easy familiarity that
it never seemed strange to come on young boys droning
their lessons under the long twisted yellow flytrap hung
from the ceiling, the *shammes*, the sexton, waddling about
in his carpet slippers carrying a fly swatter, mumbling old
Hebrew tunes to himself—*Ái! Bái! Biddle Bái Dóm!*—as he
dashed after a fly, while his wife, whom we mockingly

called the *rebbitsin*, the rabbi's wife, red-faced over her
pots in the kitchen next door, shrieked curses against the
boys playing punchball in the street—*bandits* and *murder-
ers*, she would call the police!—who were always just about
to break her windows. The wood in the benches and in
the high desk before the Ark had taken on with age and
long use such a deep rosy mirror shine that on those afternoons when I strayed in on my way back from school, I
would think that if only I bent over it long enough I might
see my own face reflected in the wood. I never did. Secretly, I thought the synagogue a mean place, and went
only because I was expected to. Whenever I crossed the
splintered and creaking porch into that stale air of snuff,
of old men and old books, and saw the dusty gilt brocade
on the prayer shawls, I felt I was being pulled into some
mysterious and ancient clan that claimed me as its own
simply because I had been born a block away. Whether
I agreed with its beliefs or not, I belonged; whether I as-
sented to its rights over me or not, I belonged; whatever
I thought of them, no matter how far I might drift from
that place, I belonged. This was understood in the very
nature of things; I was a Jew. It did not matter how little
I knew or understood of the faith, or that I was always
reading alien books; I belonged, I had been expected, I
was now to take my place in the great tradition.

For several months before my confirmation at thirteen,
I appeared every Wednesday afternoon before a choleric
old *melamed*, a Hebrew teacher, who would sit across the
table eating peas, and with an incredulous scowl on his face
listen to me go over and over the necessary prayers and
invocations, slapping me sharply on the hands whenever

I stammered on a syllable. I had to learn many passages by heart, but never understood most of them, nor was I particularly expected to understand them; it was as if some contract in secret cipher had been drawn up between the Lord of Hosts and Gita Fayge's son Alfred which that *Amerikaner idiót*, as the *melamed* called me, could sign with an x. In the "old country" the *melamed* might possibly have encouraged me to understand the text, might even have discussed it with me. Here it was understood that I would go through the lessons simply for form's sake, because my mother wished to see me confirmed; the *melamed* expected nothing more of me. In his presence I stammered more wildly than ever, and on each line. *"Idiót!"* he would scream. "They have produced an *idiót* in you, *idiót!"* Sitting back in his chair, he would hear me out with a look of contemptuous resignation as I groaned and panted my way to the end of each passage, heave sighs of disgust at the ceiling, and mechanically take up some peas to throw them into his mouth one by one, always ready to lean across the table with his bitter smile and slap my hands.

Still, I had to go through with it; I was a Jew. Yet it puzzled me that no one around me seemed to take God very seriously. We neither believed nor disbelieved. He was our oldest habit. For me, He was horribly the invisible head above the Board of Superintendents, the Almighty Judge Who watched you in every thought and deed, and to Whom I prayed for help in passing midterms and finals, His prophetess Deborah leading me safely through so long as I remembered to say under my breath as I walked in the street, *"Desolate were the open towns in Israel, they were desolate, until that I arose, Deborah."* He filled my world with unceasing dread; He had such power over me, watched me so unrelentingly, that it puzzled me to think He had to watch all the others with the same care; one night I dreamed of Him as a great engineer in some glass-walled control tower high in the sky glaring fixedly at a brake on which my name alone was written. In some ways He was simply a mad tyrant, someone I needed constantly to propitiate. Deborah alone would know how to intercede for me. Then He became a good-luck piece I carried around to get me the things I needed. I resented this God of Israel and of the Board of Superintendents; He would never let me rest.

I could not even speak of Him to others—not to the aged and bearded men in the synagogue always smelling of snuff, who spoke of the Talmud with a complacent little smile on their faces; not to the young Zionist pioneers in their clubhouses off Pitkin Avenue, who were busily learning to be farmers in the Land of Israel and chilled me with that same complacency whenever they formed their lips around the word *Jew;* certainly not to those strangers standing on the steps of the little Protestant church on Rockaway or to the Italians in the new red-brick Catholic church just off East New York Avenue, at the borders of Brownsville. He was my private burden, my peculiar misfortune.

Yet I never really wanted to give Him up. In some way it would have been hopeless to justify to myself—I had feared Him so long—He fascinated me, He seemed to hold the solitary place I most often went back to. There was a particular sensation connected with this—not of peace, not of certainty, not of goodness—but of depth; as if it were there I felt right to myself at last.

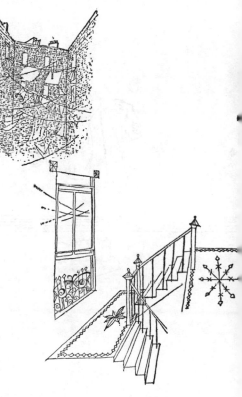

THE KITCHEN

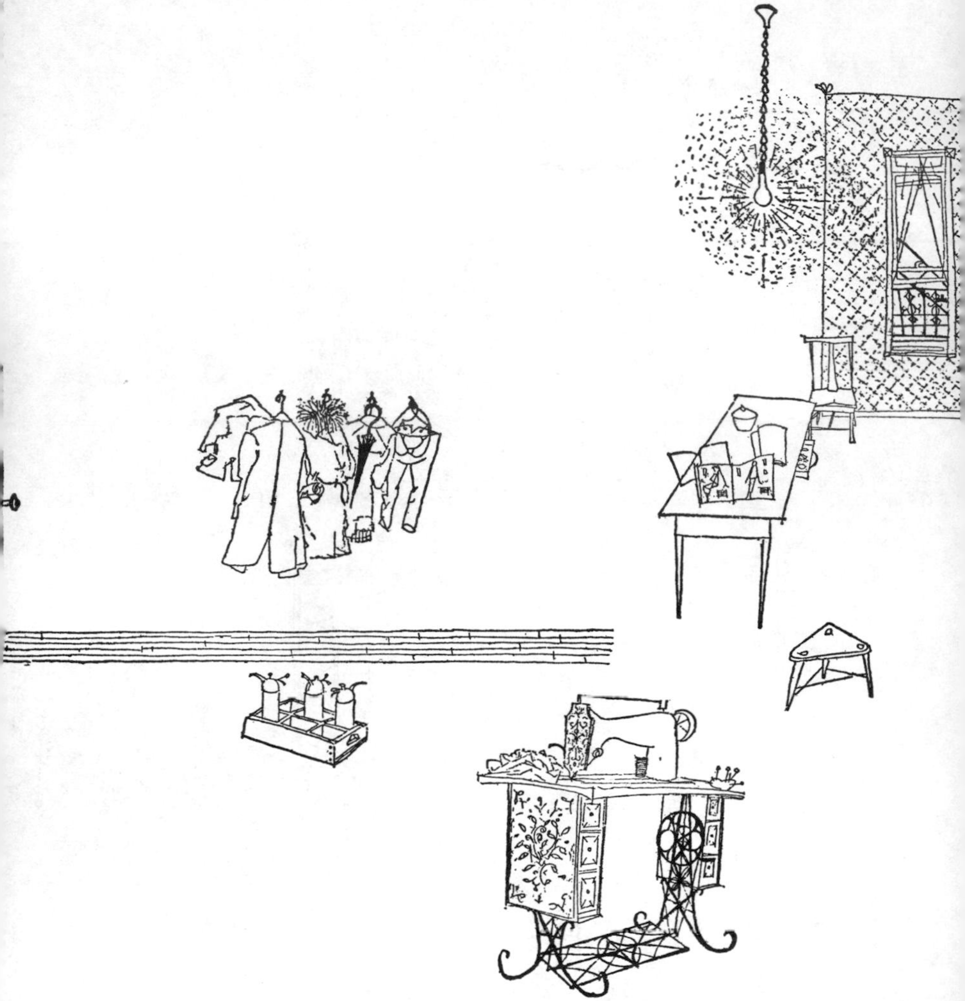

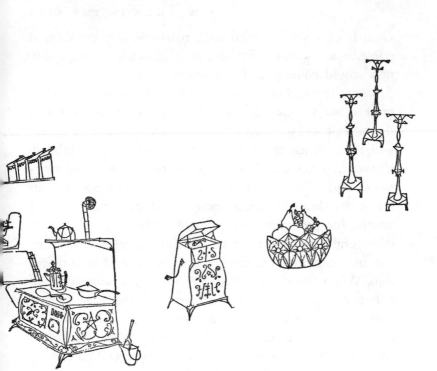

THE LAST TIME I saw our kitchen this clearly was one afternoon in London at the end of the war, when I waited out the rain in the entrance to a music store. A radio was playing into the street, and standing there I heard a broadcast of the first Sabbath service from Belsen Concentration Camp. When the liberated Jewish prisoners recited the *Hear O Israel, the Lord Our God, the Lord is*

One, I felt myself carried back to the Friday evenings at home, when with the Sabbath at sundown a healing quietness would come over Brownsville.

It was the darkness and emptiness of the streets I liked most about Friday evening, as if in preparation for that day of rest and worship which the Jews greet "as a bride" —that day when the very touch of money is prohibited, all work, all travel, all household duties, even to the turning on and off of a light—Jewry had found its way past its tormented heart to some ancient still center of itself. I waited for the streets to go dark on Friday evening as other children waited for the Christmas lights. Even Friday morning after the tests were over glowed in anticipation. When I returned home after three, the warm odor of a coffee cake baking in the oven and the sight of my mother on her hands and knees scrubbing the linoleum on the dining room floor filled me with such tenderness that I could feel my senses reaching out to embrace every single object in our household. One Friday, after a morning in school spent on the voyages of Henry Hudson, I returned with the phrase *Among the discoverers of the New World* singing in my mind as the theme of my own new-found freedom on the Sabbath.

My great moment came at six, when my father returned from work, his overalls smelling faintly of turpentine and shellac, white drops of silver paint still gleaming on his chin. Hanging his overcoat in the long dark hall that led into our kitchen, he would leave in one pocket a loosely folded copy of the New York *World;* and then everything that beckoned to me from that other hemisphere of my brain beyond the East River would start up from the smell of fresh newsprint and the sight of the globe on the front page. It was a paper that carried special associations for me with Brooklyn Bridge. They published the *World* under the green dome on Park Row overlooking the bridge; the fresh salt air of New York harbor lingered for me in the smell of paint and damp newsprint in the hall. I felt that my father brought the outside straight into our house with each day's copy of the *World*. The bridge somehow stood for freedom; the *World* for that rangy kindness and fraternalism and ease we found in Heywood Broun. My father would read aloud from "It Seems To Me" with a delighted smile on his face. "A very clear and courageous man!" he would say. "Look how he stands up for our Sacco and Vanzetti! A real social conscience, that man! Practically a Socialist!" Then, taking off his overalls, he would wash up at the kitchen sink, peeling and gnawing the paint off his nails with Gold Dust Washing Powder as I poured it into his hands, smacking his lips and grunting with pleasure as he washed himself clean of the job at last, and making me feel that I was really helping him, that I, too, was contributing to the greatness of the evening and the coming day.

By sundown the streets were empty, the curtains had been drawn, the world put to rights. Even the kitchen walls had been scrubbed and now gleamed in the Sabbath candles. On the long white tablecloth were the "company" dishes, filled for some with *gefillte* fish on lettuce leaves, ringed by red horseradish, sour and half-sour pickles, tomato salad with a light vinegar dressing; for others, with chopped liver in a bed of lettuce leaves and white radishes; the long white *khalleh*, the Sabbath loaf;

chicken soup with noodles *and* dumplings; chicken, meat loaf, prunes, and sweet potatoes that had been baked all day into an open pie; compote of prunes and quince, apricots and orange rind; applesauce; a great brown nutcake filled with almonds, the traditional *lekakh;* all surrounded by glasses of port wine, seltzer bottles with their nozzles staring down at us waiting to be pressed; a samovar of Russian tea, *svetouchnee* from the little red box, always served in tall glasses, with lemon slices floating on top. My father and mother sipped it in Russian fashion, through lumps of sugar held between the teeth.

Afterwards we went into the "dining room" and, since we were not particularly orthodox, allowed ourselves little pleasures outside the Sabbath rule—an occasional game of Casino at the dining-room table where we never dined; and listening to the victrola. The evening was particularly good for me whenever the unmarried cousin who boarded with us had her two closest friends in after supper.

They were all dressmakers, like my mother; had worked with my mother in the same East Side sweatshops; were all passionately loyal members of the International Ladies Garment Workers Union; and were all unmarried. We were their only family. Despite my mother's frenzied matchmaking, she had never succeeded in pinning a husband down for any of them. As she said, they were all too *particular*—what a calamity for a Jewish woman to remain unmarried! But my cousin and her friends accepted their fate calmly, and prided themselves on their culture and their strong *progressive* interests. They felt they belonged not to the "kitchen world," like my mother, but to the enlightened tradition of the old Russian intelligentsia.

Whenever my mother sighed over them, they would smile out of their greater knowledge of the world, and looking at me with a pointed appeal for recognition, would speak of novels they had read in Yiddish and Russian, of *Winesburg, Ohio*, of some article in the *Nation*.

Our cousin and her two friends were of my parents' generation, but I could never believe it—they seemed to enjoy life with such outspokenness. They were the first grown-up people I had ever met who used the word *love* without embarrassment. "*Libbe! Libbe!*" my mother would explode whenever one of them protested that she could not, after all, marry a man she did not love. "What is this love you make such a stew about? You do not like the way he holds his cigarette? Marry him first and it will all come out right in the end!" It astonished me to realize there was a world in which even unmarried women no longer young were simply individual human beings with lives of their own. *Our* parents, whatever affection might offhandedly be expressed between them, always had the look of being committed to something deeper than *mere* love. Their marriages were neither happy nor unhappy; they were arrangements. However they had met —whether in Russia or in the steerage or, like my parents, in an East Side boarding house—whatever they still thought of each other, *love* was not a word they used easily. Marriage was an institution people entered into— for all I could ever tell—only from immigrant loneliness, a need to be with one's own kind that mechanically resulted in the *family*. The *family* was a whole greater than all the individuals who made it up, yet made sense only in their untiring solidarity. I was perfectly sure that in my parents' minds *libbe* was something exotic and not wholly legitimate, reserved for "educated" people like their children, who were the sole end of their existence. My father and mother worked in a rage to put us above their level; they had married to make *us* possible. We were the only conceivable end to all their striving; we were their America.

So far as I knew, love was not an element admissible in my parents' experience. Any open talk of it between themselves would have seemed ridiculous. It would have suggested a wicked self-indulgence, a preposterous attention to one's own feelings, possible only to those who were free enough to choose. They did not consider themselves free. They were awed by us, as they were awed by their own imagined unworthiness, and looked on themselves only as instruments toward the ideal "American" future that would be lived by their children. As poor immigrants who had remained in Brownsville, painfully conscious of the *alrightniks* on Eastern Parkway—oh, those successes of whom I was always hearing so much, and whom we admired despite all our socialism!—everything in their lives combined to make them look down on love as something *they* had no time for. Of course there was a deep resentment in this, and when on those Friday evenings our cousin or her two friends openly mentioned the unheard-of collapse of someone's marriage—

"Sórelle and Berke? I don't believe it."

"But it's true."

"You must be joking!"

"No, it's true!"

"You're joking! You're joking!"

"No, it's true!"

—I noticed that my parents' talk had an unnaturally hard edge to it, as if those who gave themselves up to love must inevitably come to grief. Love, they could have said, was not *serious*. Life was a battle to "make sure"; it had no place, as we had no time, for whims.

Love, in fact, was something for the movies, which my parents enjoyed, but a little ashamedly. They were the land of the impossible. On those few occasions when my mother closed her sewing machine in the evening and allowed herself a visit to the Supreme, or the Palace, or the Premier, she would return, her eyes gleaming with wonder and some distrust at the strangeness of it all, to report on erotic fanatics who were, thank God, like no one we knew. What heedlessness! What daring! What riches! To my mother riches alone were the gateway to romance, for only those who had money enough could afford the freedom, and the crazy boldness, to give themselves up to love.

Yet there they were in our own dining room, our cousin and her two friends—women, grown-up women—talking openly of the look on Garbo's face when John Gilbert took her in his arms, serenely disposing of each new *khayimyankel*, poor wretch, my mother had picked for them, and arguing my father down on small points of Socialist doctrine. As they sat around the cut-glass bowl on the table—cracking walnuts, expertly peeling the skin off an apple in long even strips, cozily sipping at a glass of tea—they crossed their legs in comfort and gave off a deliciously musky fragrance of face powder that instantly framed them for me in all their dark coloring, brilliantly white teeth, and the rosy Russian blouses that swelled and rippled in terraces of embroidery over their opulent breasts.

They had a great flavor for me, those three women: they were the positive center of that togetherness that always meant so much to me in our dining room on Friday evenings. It was a quality that seemed to start in the prickly thickness of the cut-glass bowl laden with nuts and fruits; in the light from the long black-shaded lamp hanging over the table as it shimmered against the thick surfaces of the bowl and softened that room where the lace curtains were drawn against the dark and empty streets—and then found its unexpectedly tender voice in the Yiddish folksongs and Socialist hymns they taught me—*"Let's Now Forgive Each Other"*; *"Tsuzamen, Tsuzamen, All Together, Brothers!"* Those Friday evenings, I suddenly found myself enveloped in some old, primary Socialist idea that men could go beyond every barrier of race and nation and language, even of class! into some potential loving union of the whole human race. I was suddenly glad to be a Jew, as these women were Jews —simply and naturally glad of those Jewish dressmakers who spoke with enthusiastic familiarity of Sholem Aleichem and Peretz, Gorky and Tolstoy, who glowed at every reminiscence of Nijinsky, of Nazimova in *The Cherry Orchard*, of Pavlova in "The Swan."

Often, those Friday evenings, they spoke of *der heym,* "Home," and then it was hard for me. *Heym* was a terrible word. I saw millions of Jews lying dead under the Polish eagle with knives in their throats. I was afraid with my mother's fears, thought I should weep when she wept, lived again through every pogrom whose terrors she chanted. I associated with that old European life only pain, mud, and hopelessness, but I was of it still, through her. Whenever she would call through the roll of her many brothers and sisters and their children, remembering at each name that this one was dead, that one dead, another starving and sure soon to die—who knew *how* they were living these days in that miserable Poland?—I felt there was some supernatural Polish eagle across the sea whose face I should never see, but which sent out dark electrical rays to hold me fast.

In many ways *der heym* was entirely dim and abstract, nothing to do with me at all, alien as the skullcap and beard and frock coat of my mother's father, whom I never saw, but whose calm orthodox dignity stared up at me from an old cracked photograph at the bottom of the bureau drawer. Yet I lived each of my mother's fears from Dugschitz to Hamburg to London to Hester Street to Brownsville through and through with such fidelity that there were times when I wished I had made that journey too, wished I could have seen Czarist Russia, since I had in any event to suffer it all over again. I often felt odd twinges of jealousy because my parents could talk about that more intense, somehow less *experimental* life than ours with so many private smiles between themselves. It was bewildering, it made me long constantly to get at some past nearer my own New York life, my having to live with all those running wounds of a world I had never seen.

Then, under cover of the talk those Friday evenings, I would take up *The Boy's Life of Theodore Roosevelt* again, and moodily call out to those strangers on the summer veranda in Oyster Bay until my father spoke *his* tale of arriving in America. That was hard, too, painful in another way—yet it always made him curiously lighthearted and left me swimming in space. For he had gone off painting box cars on the Union Pacific, had been as far west as Omaha, had actually seen Sidney Hillman toiling in Hart, Schaffner and Marx's Chicago factory, had heard his beloved Debs making fools of Bryan and Taft in the 1908 campaign, had been offered a homestead in Colorado! *Omaha* was the most beautiful word I had ever heard, *homestead* almost as beautiful; but I could never forgive him for not having accepted that homestead.

"What would I have done there? I'm no farmer."

"You should have taken it! Why do we always live here!"

"It would have been too lonely. Nobody I knew."

"What a chance!"

"Don't be childish. Nobody I knew."

"Why? Why?"

"Alfred, what do you want of us poor Jews?"

So it was: we had always to be together: believers and non-believers, we were a people; I was of that people. Unthinkable to go one's own way, to doubt or to escape the fact that I was a Jew. I had heard of Jews who pretended they were not, but could not understand them. We had all of us lived together so long that we would not have known how to separate even if we had wanted to. The most terrible word was *aleyn*, alone. I always had the same picture of a man desolately walking down a dark street, newspapers and cigarette butts contemptuously fly-

ing in his face as he tasted in the dusty grit the full
measure of his strangeness. *Aleyn! Aleyn!* My father had
been alone here in America as a boy. *His* father, whose
name I bore, had died here at twenty-five of pneumonia
caught on a garment workers' picket line, and his body
flung in with thousands of other Jews who had perished
those first years on the East Side. My father had never
been able to find his father's grave. *Aleyn! Aleyn!* Did
immigrant Jews, then, marry only out of loneliness? Was
even Socialism just a happier way of keeping us together?

I trusted it to do that. Socialism would be one long
Friday evening around the samovar and the cut-glass bowl
laden with nuts and fruits, all of us singing *Tsuzamen,
tsuzamen, ale tsuzamen!* Then the heroes of the Russian
novel—*our* kind of people—would walk the world, and I
—still wearing a circle-necked Russian blouse *"à la
Tolstoy"*—would live forever with those I loved in that
beautiful Russian country of the mind. Listening to our
cousin and her two friends I, who had never seen it, who
associated with it nothing but the names of great writers
and my father's saying as we went through the Brooklyn
Botanic Garden—"Nice! but you should have seen the
Czar's summer palace at Tsarskoye-Selo!"—suddenly saw
Russia as the grand antithesis to all bourgeois ideals, the
spiritual home of all truly free people. I was perfectly
sure that there was no literature in the world like the
Russian; that the only warm hearts in the world were
Russian, like our cousin and her two friends; that other
people were always dully materialist, but that the Russian
soul, like Nijinsky's dream of pure flight, would always
leap outward, past all barriers, to a lyric world in which

my ideal socialism and the fiery moodiness of Tchaikov-
sky's *Pathétique* would be entirely at home with each
other. *Tsuzamen, alle tsuzamen!* How many millions
would be with us! China was in our house those Friday
evenings, Africa, the Indian masses. And it was those three
unmarried dressmakers from the rank and file who fully
wrapped me in that spell, with the worldly clang of their
agate beads and the musky fragrance of their face powder
and their embroidered Russian blouses, with the great
names of Russian writers ringing against the cut-glass bowl
under the black lamp. Never did the bowl look so laden,
never did apples and tea smell so good, never did the
samovar pour out with such steaming bounty, as on those
Friday evenings when I tasted in the tea and the talk the
evangelical heart of our cousin and her two friends, and
realized that it was we—we!—who would someday put
the world on its noblest course.

"*Kinder, kinder,*" my mother would say. "Enough
discusye. Maybe now a little music? Alfred, play *Sche-
herazade!*"

You could melt their hearts with it; the effect of the
violin on almost everyone I knew was uncanny. I could
watch them softening, easing, already on the brink of
tears—yet with their hands at rest in their laps, they stared
straight ahead at the wall, breathing hard, an unforeseen
smile of rapture on their mouths. Any slow movement, if
only it were played lingeringly and sagely enough, seemed
to come to them as a reminiscence of a reminiscence. It
seemed to have something to do with our being Jews. The
depths of Jewish memory the violin could throw open
apparently had no limit—for every slow movement was

based on something "Russian," every plaintive melody
even in Beethoven or Mozart was "Jewish." I could skip
from composer to composer, from theme to theme, without any fear, ever, of being detected, for all slow move-
ments fell into a single chant of *der heym* and of the
great *Kol Nidre* sung in the first evening hours of the
Day of Atonement, in whose long rending cry—of con-
trition? of grief? of hopeless love for the Creator?—I
relived all of the Jews' bitter intimacy with death.

Then I cranked up the old brown Victor, took our
favorite records out of the red velvet pleated compart-
ments, and we listened to John McCormack singing *Ave
Maria*, Amelita Galli-Curci singing *Caro Nome* ("How
ugly she is!" my parents would say wonderingly. "Have
you seen her picture? Incredible! But how she sings!"),
and Alma Gluck singing *Comin' Thro' the Rye*. The high
point was Caruso singing from *La Juive*. He inspired in
my father and mother such helpless, intimidated adoration
that I came to think of what was always humbly referred
to as his *golden voice* as the invocation of a god. The
pleasure he gave us was beyond all music. When Mischa
Elman played some well-known melody we sighed familiarly at each other—his tone was so *warm;* he bubbled
slowly in my ears like the sound of chicken fat crackling
in the pan. But Caruso, "that *Italyéner*," seemed to me the
echo of some outrageously pagan voice at the roof of the
world. While I pushed at the hand-crank and the wheezy
sounds of the orchestra in the background came to me as
the whispered turnings, sighs and alarms of the crowd
around the circus pit, there on high, and rising higher
and higher with each note, that voice, that *golden voice*,

leaped its way from one trapeze to another. We sat hunched in our wonder, our adoration, our fear. Would he make it? Could any human being find that last impossible rung?

Rachel! Quand du Seigneur la grâce tutélaire. . . .

Then, suddenly bounding back to earth again, there he was before us again, secretly smiling, the tones welling out of him with such brazen strength, such irresistible energy, that he left us gasping. I could see him standing inside the victrola box—a centaur just out of the woods, not quite human, with that enigmatic, almost contemptuous smile on his face. "What a voice!" my father would say over and over, deeply shaken. "What a voice! It's not human! Never was there a voice like it! Only the other day I was reading that when they opened him up after he died they found his vocal chords were ab-solutely unique!" Then, his face white with pleasure, with amazement, with wonder: "Oh that *Italyéner!* Oh that *Italyéner!* What a power he has, that *Italyéner!*"

In Brownsville tenements the kitchen is always the largest room and the center of the household. As a child I felt that we lived in a kitchen to which four other rooms were annexed. My mother, a "home" dressmaker, had her workshop in the kitchen. She told me once that she had begun dressmaking in Poland at thirteen; as far back as I can remember, she was always making dresses for the local women. She had an innate sense of design, a quick eye for all the subtleties in the latest fashions, even when she despised them, and great boldness. For three or four dol-

lars she would study the fashion magazines with a customer, go with the customer to the remnants store on
Belmont Avenue to pick out the material, argue the owner
down—all remnants stores, for some reason, were supposed to be shady, as if the owners dealt in stolen goods
—and then for days would patiently fit and baste and
sew and fit again. Our apartment was always full of
women in their housedresses sitting around the kitchen
table waiting for a fitting. My little bedroom next to the
kitchen was the fitting room. The sewing machine, an
old nut-brown Singer with golden scrolls painted along
the black arm and engraved along the two tiers of little
drawers massed with needles and thread on each side of
the treadle, stood next to the window and the great coal-
black stove which up to my last year in college was our
main source of heat. By December the two outer bed-
rooms were closed off, and used to chill bottles of milk
and cream, cold borscht and jellied calves' feet.

The kitchen held our lives together. My mother worked
in it all day long, we ate in it almost all meals except the
Passover *seder*, I did my homework and first writing at
the kitchen table, and in winter I often had a bed made
up for me on three kitchen chairs near the stove. On the
wall just over the table hung a long horizontal mirror
that sloped to a ship's prow at each end and was lined in
cherry wood. It took up the whole wall, and drew every
object in the kitchen to itself. The walls were a fiercely
stippled whitewash, so often rewhitened by my father in
slack seasons that the paint looked as if it had been
squeezed and cracked into the walls. A large electric bulb
hung down the center of the kitchen at the end of a chain

that had been hooked into the ceiling; the old gas ring
and key still jutted out of the wall like antlers. In the
corner next to the toilet was the sink at which we washed,
and the square tub in which my mother did our clothes.
Above it, tacked to the shelf on which were pleasantly
ranged square, blue-bordered white sugar and spice jars,
hung calendars from the Public National Bank on Pitkin
Avenue and the Minsker Progressive Branch of the Work-
man's Circle; receipts for the payment of insurance pre-
miums, and household bills on a spindle; two little boxes
engraved with Hebrew letters. One of these was for the
poor, the other to buy back the Land of Israel. Each spring
a bearded little man would suddenly appear in our kitchen,
salute us with a hurried Hebrew blessing, empty the boxes
(sometimes with a sidelong look of disdain if they were
not full), hurriedly bless us again for remembering our
less fortunate Jewish brothers and sisters, and so take his
departure until the next spring, after vainly trying to
persuade my mother to take still another box. We did
occasionally remember to drop coins in the boxes, but
this was usually only on the dreaded morning of "midterms" and final examinations, because my mother thought
it would bring me luck. She was extremely superstitious,
but embarrassed about it, and always laughed at herself
whenever, on the morning of an examination, she coun-
seled me to leave the house on my right foot. "I know it's
silly," her smile seemed to say, "but what harm can it
do? It may calm God down."

The kitchen gave a special character to our lives; my
mother's character. All my memories of that kitchen are
dominated by the nearness of my mother sitting all day
long at her sewing machine, by the clacking of the treadle

against the linoleum floor, by the patient twist of her right shoulder as she automatically pushed at the wheel with one hand or lifted the foot to free the needle where it had got stuck in a thick piece of material. The kitchen was her life. Year by year, as I began to take in her fantastic capacity for labor and her anxious zeal, I realized it was ourselves she kept stitched together. I can never remember a time when she was not working. She worked because the law of her life was work, work and anxiety; she worked because she would have found life meaningless without work. She read almost no English; she could read the Yiddish paper, but never felt she had time to. We were always talking of a time when I would teach her how to read, but somehow there was never time. When I awoke in the morning she was already at her machine, or in the great morning crowd of housewives at the grocery getting fresh rolls for breakfast. When I returned from school she was at her machine, or conferring over *McCall's* with some neighborhood woman who had come in pointing hopefully to an illustration—"Mrs. Kazin! Mrs. Kazin! Make me a dress like it shows here in the picture!" When my father came home from work she had somehow mysteriously interrupted herself to make supper for us, and the dishes cleared and washed, was back at her machine. When I went to bed at night, often she was still there, pounding away at the treadle, hunched over the wheel, her hands steering a piece of gauze under the needle with a finesse that always contrasted sharply with her swollen hands and broken nails. Her left hand had been pierced through when as a girl she had worked in the infamous Triangle Shirtwaist Factory on the East Side. A needle had gone straight through the palm, sev-

ering a large vein. They had sewn it up for her so clumsily
that a tuft of flesh always lay folded over the palm.

The kitchen was the great machine that set our lives
running; it whirred down a little only on Saturdays and
holy days. From my mother's kitchen I gained my first
picture of life as a white, overheated, starkly lit workshop redolent with Jewish cooking, crowded with women
in housedresses, strewn with fashion magazines, patterns,
dress material, spools of thread—and at whose center, so
lashed to her machine that bolts of energy seemed to
dance out of her hands and feet as she worked, my mother
stamped the treadle hard against the floor, hard, hard, and
silently, grimly at war, beat out the first rhythm of the
world for me.

Every sound from the street roared and trembled at
our windows—a mother feeding her child on the door-
step, the screech of the trolley cars on Rockaway Avenue,
the eternal smash of a handball against the wall of our
house, the clatter of *"der Italyéner"*'s cart packed with
watermelons, the sing-song of the old-clothes men walking Chester Street, the cries *"Árbes! Árbes! Kinder!
Kinder! Heyse gute árbes!"* All day long people streamed
into our apartment as a matter of course—"customers,"
upstairs neighbors, downstairs neighbors, women who
would stop in for a half-hour's talk, salesmen, relatives,
insurance agents. Usually they came in without ringing
the bell—everyone knew my mother was always at home.
I would hear the front door opening, the wind whistling
through our front hall, and then some familiar face would
appear in our kitchen with the same bland, matter-of-fact
inquiring look: no need to stand on ceremony: my mother
and her kitchen were available to everyone all day long.

At night the kitchen contracted around the blaze of light on the cloth, the patterns, the ironing board where the iron had burned a black border around the tear in the muslin cover; the finished dresses looked so frilly as they jostled on their wire hangers after all the work my mother had put into them. And then I would get that strangely ominous smell of tension from the dress fabrics and the burn in the cover of the ironing board—as if each piece of cloth and paper crushed with light under the naked bulb might suddenly go up in flames. Whenever I pass some small tailoring shop still lit up at night and see the owner hunched over his steam press; whenever in some poorer neighborhood of the city I see through a window some small crowded kitchen naked under the harsh light glittering in the ceiling, I still smell that fiery breath, that warning of imminent fire. I was always holding my breath. What I must have felt most about ourselves, I see now, was that we ourselves were like kindling—that all the hard-pressed pieces of ourselves and all the hard-used objects in that kitchen were like so many slivers of wood that might go up in flames if we came too near the white-blazing filaments in that naked bulb. Our tension itself was fire, we ourselves were forever burning—to live, to get down the foreboding in our souls, to make good.

Twice a year, on the anniversaries of her parents' deaths, my mother placed on top of the ice-box an ordinary kitchen glass packed with wax, the *yortsayt*, and lit the candle in it. Sitting at the kitchen table over my homework, I would look across the threshold to that mourning-glass, and sense that for my mother the distance from our kitchen to *der heym*, from life to death, was only a flame's length away. Poor as we were, it was not poverty that drove my mother so hard; it was loneliness—some endless bitter brooding over all those left behind, dead or dying or soon to die; a loneliness locked up in her kitchen that dwelt every day on the hazardousness of life and the nearness of death, but still kept struggling in the lock, trying to get us through by endless labor.

With us, life started up again only on the last shore. There seemed to be no middle ground between despair and the fury of our ambition. Whenever my mother spoke of her hopes for us, it was with such unbelievingness that the likes of us would ever come to anything, such abashed hope and readiness for pain, that I finally came to see in the flame burning on top of the ice-box death itself burning away the bones of poor Jews, burning out in us everything but courage, the blind resolution to live. In the light of that mourning-candle, there were ranged around me how many dead and dying—how many eras of pain, of exile, of dispersion, of cringing before the powers of this world!

It was always at dusk that my mother's loneliness came home most to me. Painfully alert to every shift in the light at her window, she would suddenly confess her fatigue by removing her pince-nez, and then wearily pushing aside the great mound of fabrics on her machine, would stare at the street as if to warm herself in the last of the sun. "How sad it is!" I once heard her say. "It grips me! It grips me!" Twilight was the bottommost part of the day, the chillest and loneliest time for her. Always so near to her moods, I knew she was fighting some deep inner dread, struggling against the returning tide of darkness along the streets that invariably assailed her heart with the same foreboding— Where? Where now? Where is the day taking us now?

Yet one good look at the street would revive her. I
see her now, perched against the windowsill, with her
face against the glass, her eyes almost asleep in enjoyment,
just as she starts up with the guilty cry—"What foolish-
ness is this in me!"—and goes to the stove to prepare supper for us: a moment, only a moment, watching the evening crowd of women gathering at the grocery for fresh
bread and milk. But between my mother's pent-up face
at the window and the winter sun dying in the fabrics—
"Alfred, see how beautiful!"—she has drawn for me one
single line of sentience.

The unmarried cousin who boarded with us had English books in her room—the only English books in our
house I did not bring into it myself. Half an hour before
supper, I liked nothing better than to stray into her room,
and sitting on the India print spread of her bed next to the
yellow wicker bookstand, look through her books and
smell the musky face powder that filled her room. There
was no closet: her embroidered Russian blouses and red
velvet suits hung behind a curtain, and the lint seemed
to float off the velvet and swim in multicolored motes
through the air. On the wall over her bed hung a picture
of two half-nude lovers fleeing from a storm, and an oval-
framed picture of Psyche perched on a rock. On the
wicker bookstand, in a star-shaped frame of thick glass,
was a photograph of our cousin's brother, missing since
the Battle of Tannenberg, in the uniform of a Czarist
Army private.

In that wicker bookstand, below the blue set of Sholem

Aleichem in Yiddish and the scattered volumes of Russian novels, were the books I would never have to drag
from the Stone Avenue Library myself—THE WORLD'S
GREATEST SELECTED SHORT STORIES; a biography of Alfred
E. Smith entitled *Up From the City Streets;* a Grosset
and Dunlap edition of *The Sheik;* and in English, a volume of stories by Alexander Kuprin. Day after day at
five-thirty, half an hour before supper, I would sit myself
carefully on the India print, and fondle those books with
such rapture that they were actually *there,* for me to look
through whenever I liked, that on some days I could not
bear to open them at all, but sat as close to the sun in the
windows as I could, breathing the lint in, and the sun still
hot on the India spread.

On the roof just across the street, the older boys now
home from work would spring their pigeons from the
traps. You could see the feathers glistening faintly in the
last light, beating thinly against their sides—they, too,
sucking air as the birds leaped up from their wire cages.
Then, widening and widening their flight each time they
came over our roof again, they went round a sycamore
and the spire of the church without stopping. The sun
fell straight on the India spread—how the thin prickly
material burned in my nostrils—and glowed along the bony
gnarled bumps in the legs of the yellow wicker bookstand. Happiness was warmth. Beyond Chester Street, beyond even Rockaway, I could see to where the Italians
lived on broken streets that rose up to a hill topped by a
church. The church seemed to be thickly surrounded by
trees. In his star-shaped glass on the bookstand, that Russian soldier missing since the Battle of Tannenberg looked
steadily at me from under his round forage cap. His chest

bulged against two rows of gold buttons up and down his black blouse. Where? Where now? Had they put him, too, into a great pit? Suddenly it did not matter. Happiness was the sun on the India spread, the hot languid sands lapping at the tent of the Sheik—"*Monseigneur! My desert prince!*"—the summer smell of the scum on the East River just off Oliver Street where Alfred E. Smith worked in the Fulton Fish Market. In the Kuprin stories an old man and a boy went wandering up a road in the Crimea. There was dust on the road, dust on the leaves— *hoo! hoo! my son! how it is hot!* But they were happy. It was summer in the Crimea, and just to walk along with them made me happy. When they got hungry they stopped at a spring, took black bread, salt, and tomatoes out of their knapsacks, and ate. The ripe open tomatoes gushed red from their mouths, the black bread and salt were good, very good, and when they leaned over to drink at the spring, the water was so icy cold it made my teeth ache. I read that story over and over, sometimes skipping pages to get to the part about the bread, the salt, the tomatoes, the icy water. *I could taste that bread, that salt, those tomatoes, that icy spring.*

Now the light begins to die. Twilight is also the mind's grazing time. Twilight is the bottom of that arc down which we had fallen the whole long day, but where I now sit at our cousin's window in some strange silence of attention, watching the pigeons go round and round to the leafy smell of soupgreens from the stove. In the cool of that first evening hour, as I sit at the table waiting for supper and my father and the New York *World*, everything is so rich to overflowing, I hardly know where to begin.

THE BLOCK

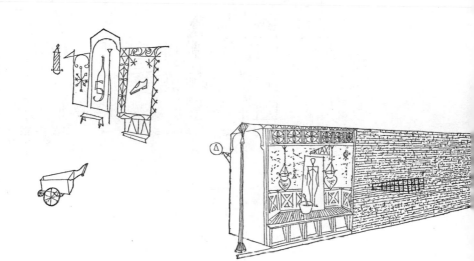

AND BEYOND

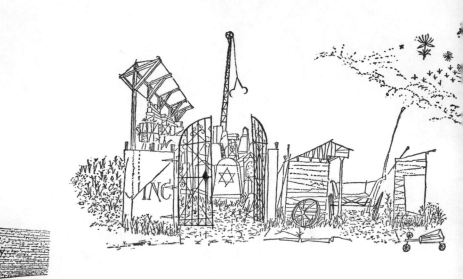

THE OLD DRUGSTORE on our corner has been replaced by a second-hand furniture store; the old candy store has been replaced by a second-hand furniture store, the old bakery, the old hardware shop, the old "coffee pot" that was once reached over a dirt road. I was there the day they put a pavement in. That "coffee pot" was the first restaurant I ever sat in, trembling—they served ham and bacon there—over a swiss cheese on rye and coffee in a thick mug without a saucer as I watched the truck drivers kidding the heavily lipsticked girl behind the counter. The whole block is now thick with second-hand furniture stores. The fluttering red canvas signs BARGAINS BARGAINS reach up to the first-floor windows. At every step I have to fight maple love seats bulging out of the doors. It looks as if our old life has been turned out into the street, suddenly reminds me of the nude shamed look furniture on the street always had those terrible first winters of the depression, when we stood around each newly evicted family to give them comfort and the young Communists raged up and down the street calling for volunteers to put the furniture back and crying aloud with their fists lifted to the sky. But on the Chester Street side of the house I make out the letters we carefully pasted there in tar sometime in the fall of either 1924 or 1925:

DAZZY VANCE

WORLDS GREATEST PICHER

262 STRIKEOUTS

BROOKLYN NATIONAL LEAG

GIANTS STINK ON ICE

DAZZY DAZZY DAZZY

The old barbershop is still there. Once it was owned by two brothers, the younger one fat and greasy and with a waxed stiffly pointed mustache of which he was so proud that he put a photograph of himself in the window with the inscription: "MEN! LOOK AT OUR MUSTACHE AND LOOK AT YOURS!" The older one was dry and sad, the "conscientious" partner. The fat brother had an old fiddle he let me play in the shop when business was bad; he would sprawl in the first barber chair languidly admiring himself in the great mirrors, clicking his teeth over the nudes in the *Police Gazette*, and keep time for me by waving his razor. I never liked him very much; he was what we reproachfully called a "sport," a loud and boastful man; he always smelled of hair lotion. You could see each hair as it ran off the crown of his head so sticky and twisted in lotion that it reflected the light from the bulbs in the ceiling. We were all a little afraid of him. One day he bought a motorcycle on credit, and as he started it from the curb, flew into the window of the delicatessen store. I remember the shiver of the glass as it instantaneously fell out all around him, and as he picked himself up, his face and hands streaming with blood, the sly little smile with which he pointed to the sausages and pickle pots in the street: "Hey you little bastards! Free treat!"

I see the barbershop through the steam from the hot towel fount. The vapor glistened on the unbelievable breasts of the calendar nudes pasted above the mirrors and on the fat bandaged chin of Peaches Browning every day in the *News* and on the great colored drawing all over the front page of the *Graphic* one morning showing Mrs. Ruth Snyder strapped and burning in the electric chair. The smell of hair tonic could never disguise the steaming exhalation of raw female flesh. Everything in that barbershop promised me a first look. On the table, along with the *News* and the *Graphic*, *College Humor* and the *Police Gazette*, lay several volumes of a pictorial history of the World War. I played the barber's violin for him only because I could then get to sit over those volumes by the hour, lost in the gray photographs and drawings of men going into battle, ruined towns in Serbia, Belgium, and France where one chimney still rose from a house destroyed by shell fire, pictures of the victorious French in 1919 dipping their battle standards in the Rhine. There were two photographs I remember particularly: it was really for them that I went back and back to that barbershop. One showed a group of German officers in full uniform, with all their medals, standing outside a brothel in France with the ladies of the house, who were naked to the waist and wore crosses between their enormous breasts. The officers had their arms comfortably draped over the girls' shoulders, and grinned into the camera. GERMAN KULTUR, ran the caption. HOW THE ENEMY AMUSES ITSELF BEHIND THE LINES. The other photograph showed Kaiser Wilhelm with his retinue, inspecting troops. The Kaiser and the generals were walking on wooden planks; the caption noted that the planks had been laid there to keep the distinguished company from walking in the blood that ran over the field.

The shoemaker is still there; the old laundry is now a printing shop. Next to it is the twin of our old house, connected with ours below the intervening stores by a long common cellar. As I look at the iron grillwork over the glass door, I think of the dark-faced girl who used to stand on that stoop night after night watching for her Italian boy friend. Her widowed mother, dressed always in black, a fat meek woman with a clubfoot, was so horrified by the affair that she went to the neighbors for help. The quarrels of mother and daughter could be heard all over the street. "How can you go around with an

Italian? How can you think of it? You're unnatural!
You're draining the blood straight from my heart!" Night
after night she would sit at her window, watching the
girl go off with her *Italyéner*—ominous word that con-
tained all her fear of the Gentiles—and weep. The Italian
boy was devoted to the daughter and wanted them to
marry. Again and again he tried to persuade the mother,
but she would lock the door on him and cry out from
behind it in Yiddish: "I have harmed you and your family?
I interfere with *your* customs? Go away and leave us be!
Leave us be! A Jewish girl is not for you, Mister! Go
away!" In desperation, he offered "to become a Jew."
No one had ever heard of such a thing, and the mother
was so astonished that she gave her consent to the marriage. The boy was overjoyed—but waited until the last
possible moment before the wedding to undergo circum-
cision, and as he walked tremblingly to the canopy, the
blood dripping down his trouser legs, fainted dead away.
The block never stopped talking about it.

Where now is my beautiful Mrs. Baruch, the "chicken
lady," who sat smack in the middle of her store on a
bloody kitchen chair plucking and plucking the feathers
off her chickens with such a raw hearty laugh that you
could hear her a block away? I would stop in her doorway on my way back from school just to watch her work,
for as she plucked, plucked the feathers off her chickens
with one grimly impatient pull along her right elbow, she
seemed instantaneously to draw out of their bellies a great
coiling mass of intestines and blood vessels, and—never

for a moment letting up in her unending hoarse cackle—
scolded and gossiped with the women standing around her.
Whenever she looked up and saw me standing in the doorway, she would hold up her hands in mock dismay,
feathers sticking to each finger, and her hairy chin trembling with laughter, would call out—"Hey, studént! My
Alfred! Come give me a big kiss! Is all right! Your mother
left here an hour ago!"

And where is Blumka, our local madwoman, who every
Friday afternoon just before the Sabbath began, icy pale
under her sleek black pompadour, made the rounds of
the block dragging a child's cart behind her and wearing
a long satin dress? She often sat on the stoop of our house
with her head resting against the glass in the door, gossiping with the neighbors or talking to herself, and never
budged until the cart was heaped with charcoal, chicory,
the long white Sabbath *khalleh*, and fruit. It was on our
steps particularly that she liked to take her rest. Perhaps
she enjoyed embarrassing us; perhaps, I used to think, she
stopped there because she knew how much I loved watching her, for she would smile and smile at me with a fixed
and shameless grin. Shameless was our word for her—a
Jewish woman to beg in the streets! She had a brutal di-
rectness in the way she did everything—flopped around
the streets all Friday long with her cart ignoring everyone
with a dreamy contempt unless she wanted to talk; openly
demanded her living of us; sat herself down on a stoop
whenever she liked, mumbling to herself or jeering at the
children; and when she liked, lay flat on the steps singing
old Yiddish ditties to herself. Always in the same long
black satin dress that came down to her high button shoes,

always dragging that battered children's cart behind her, she would sometimes lie there against the glass, her tightly coiled mass of dead-looking hair splitting the light where she lay, her long straight nose and fierce jaw jutting into the air with a kind of insolent defiance. She seemed always to be jeering, but it was hard to find out what she meant by it, for she said everything that came into her mind in the same gruff oddly disdainful tone of voice, her icy pale cheeks moving tensely up and down as she chewed at a piece of bread.

The block: *my* block. It was on the Chester Street side of our house, between the grocery and the back wall of the old drugstore, that I was hammered into the shape of the streets. Everything beginning at Blake Avenue would always wear for me some delightful strangeness and mildness, simply because it was not of my block, *the* block, where the clang of your head sounded against the pavement when you fell in a fist fight, and the rows of storelights on each side were pitiless, watching you. Anything away from the block was good: even a school you never went to, two blocks away: there were vegetable gardens in the park across the street. Returning from "New York," I would take the longest routes home from the subway, get off a station ahead of our own, only for the unexpectedness of walking through Betsy Head Park and hearing the gravel crunch under my feet as I went beyond the vegetable gardens, smelling the sweaty sweet dampness from the pool in summer and the dust on the leaves as I passed under the ailanthus trees. On the block itself everything rose up only to test me.

We worked every inch of it, from the cellars and the backyards to the sickening space between the roofs. Any wall, any stoop, any curving metal edge on a billboard sign made a place against which to knock a ball; any bottom rung of a fire escape ladder a goal in basketball; any sewer cover a base; any crack in the pavement a "net" for the tense sharp tennis that we played by beating a soft ball back and forth with our hands between the squares. Betsy Head Park two blocks away would always feel slightly foreign, for it belonged to the Amboys and the Bristols and the Hopkinsons as much as it did to us. *Our* life every day was fought out on the pavement and in the gutter, up against the walls of the houses and the glass fronts of the drugstore and the grocery, in and out of the fresh steaming piles of horse manure, the wheels of passing carts and automobiles, along the iron spikes of the stairway to the cellar, the jagged edge of the open garbage cans, the crumbly steps of the old farmhouses still left on one side of the street.

As I go back to the block now, and for a moment fold my body up again in its narrow arena—there, just there, between the black of the asphalt and the old women in their kerchiefs and flowered housedresses sitting on the tawny kitchen chairs—the back wall of the drugstore still rises up to test me. Every day we smashed a small black viciously hard regulation handball against it with fanatical cuts and drives and slams, beating and slashing at it almost in hatred for the blind strength of the wall itself. I was never good enough at handball, was always practicing

some trick shot that might earn me esteem, and when I
was weary of trying, would often bat a ball down Chester
Street just to get myself to Blake Avenue. I have this
memory of playing one-o'-cat by myself in the sleepy
twilight, at a moment when everyone else had left the
block. The sparrows floated down from the telephone
wires to peck at every fresh pile of horse manure, and
there was a smell of brine from the delicatessen store, of
egg crates and of the milk scum left in the great metal
cans outside the grocery, of the thick white paste oozing
out from behind the fresh Hecker's Flour ad on the metal
signboard. I would throw the ball in the air, hit it with
my bat, then with perfect satisfaction drop the bat to
the ground and run to the next sewer cover. Over and
over I did this, from sewer cover to sewer cover, until I
had worked my way to Blake Avenue and could see the
park.

With each clean triumphant ring of my bat against
the gutter leading me on, I did the whole length of our
block up and down, and never knew how happy I was
just watching the asphalt rise and fall, the curve of the
steps up to an old farmhouse. The farmhouses themselves
were streaked red on one side, brown on the other, but
the steps themselves were always gray. There was a tremor
of pleasure at one place; I held my breath in nausea at
another. As I ran after my ball with the bat heavy in my
hand, the odd successiveness of things in myself almost
choked me, the world was so full as I ran—past the cob-
blestoned yards into the old farmhouses, where stray
chickens still waddled along the stones; past the little
candy store where we went only if the big one on our

side of the block was out of Eskimo Pies; past the three neighboring tenements where the last of the old women sat on their kitchen chairs yawning before they went up to make supper. Then came Mrs. Rosenwasser's house, the place on the block I first identified with what was farthest from home, and strangest, because it was a "private" house; then the fences around the monument works, where black cranes rose up above the yard and you could see the smooth gray slabs that would be cut and carved into tombstones, some of them already engraved with the names and dates and family virtues of the dead.

Beyond Blake Avenue was the pool parlor outside which we waited all through the tense September afternoons of the World's Series to hear the latest scores called off the ticker tape—and where as we waited, banging a ball against the bottom of the wall and drinking water out of empty coke bottles, I breathed the chalk off the cues and listened to the clocks ringing in the fire station across the street. There was an old warehouse next to the pool parlor; the oil on the barrels and the iron staves had the same rusty smell. A block away was the park, thick with the dusty gravel I liked to hear my shoes crunch in as I ran round and round the track; then a great open pavilion, the inside mysteriously dark, chill even in summer; there I would wait in the sweaty coolness before pushing on to the wading ring where they put up a shower on the hottest days.

Beyond the park the "fields" began, all those still unused lots where we could still play hard ball in perfect peace—first shooing away the goats and then tearing up goldenrod before laying our bases. The smell and touch

of those "fields," with their wild compost under the bill-
boards of weeds, goldenrod, bricks, goat droppings, rusty
cans, empty beer bottles, fresh new lumber, and damp
cement, lives in my mind as Brownsville's great open door,
the wastes that took us through to the west. I used to go
round them in summer with my cousins selling near-beer
to the carpenters, but always in a daze, would stare so
long at the fibrous stalks of the goldenrod as I felt their
harshness in my hand that I would forget to make a sale,
and usually go off sick on the beer I drank up myself.
Beyond! Beyond! Only to see something new, to get away
from each day's narrow battleground between the grocery
and the back wall of the drugstore! Even the other end
of our block, when you got to Mrs. Rosenwasser's house
and the monument works, was dear to me for the con-
trast. On summer nights, when we played Indian trail,
running away from each other on prearranged signals, the
greatest moment came when I could plunge into the
darkness down the block for myself and hide behind the
slabs in the monument works. I remember the air whistling
around me as I ran, the panicky thud of my bones in my
sneakers, and then the slabs rising in the light from the
street lamps as I sped past the little candy store and crept
under the fence.

In the darkness you could never see where the crane
began. We liked to trap the enemy between the slabs and
sometimes jumped them from great mounds of rock just
in from the quarry. A boy once fell to his death that way,
and they put a watchman there to keep us out. This made
the slabs all the more impressive to me, and I always aimed
first for that yard whenever we played follow-the-leader.

Day after day the monument works became oppressively more mysterious and remote, though it was only just down the block; I stood in front of it every afternoon on my way back from school, filling it with my fears. It was not death I felt there—the slabs were usually faceless. It was the darkness itself, and the wind howling around me whenever I stood poised on the edge of a high slab waiting to jump. Then I would take in, along with the fear, some amazement of joy that I had found my way out that far.

Beyond! Beyond! *Beyond* was "the city," connected only by interminable subway lines and some old Brooklyn-Manhattan trolley car rattling across Manhattan Bridge. At night, as the trolley ground its way home in the rain through miles of unknown streets from some meeting in the Jewish Daily *Forward* building on the East Side to which my father had taken me, I saw the flickering light bulbs in the car, the hard yellow benches on which we sat half asleep, the motorman's figure bulging the green curtain he had drawn against the lights in the car, as a rickety cart stumbling through infinite space —the driver taking us where? *Beyond* was the wheeze of an accordion on the Staten Island ferry boat—the music rocking in such unison with the vibration of the engines as the old man walked in and out of the cars on the lower deck squeezing the tunes out of the pleats that never after would I be able to take a ferry from South Ferry, from Christopher Street, from 23rd, from Dyckman, from 125th, without expecting that same man to come round with his silver-backed accordion and his hat in his hand

as he jangled a few coins in a metal plate. *Beyond* was
the long shivering blast of the ferry starting out from
the Battery in sight of the big Colgate ad across the river
in Jersey; the depth of peace as the sun warmed the panels
of the doors sliding out to the observation deck; the old
Italian shoeshine men walking round and round with their
boxes between all those suddenly relaxed New Yorkers
comfortably staring at each other in the high wind on the
top deck; a garbage scow burning in the upper bay just
under Liberty's right arm; the minarets on Ellis Island;
the old prison walls under the trees of Governor's Island;
then, floating back in the cold dusk toward the diamond-
lighted wall of Manhattan skyscrapers, the way we huddled in the great wooden varnish-smelling cabin inside as
if we were all getting under the same quilt on a cold night.

Beyond was the canvas awnings over an El station in
summer. Inside, the florid red windows had curlicues running up and down their borders. I had never seen anything
like them in all the gritty I.R.T. stations below. Those
windows were richer than all my present. The long march
of snails up and down and around the borders of those
windows, the cursive scrolls in the middle patch forever
turning back on themselves, promised to lead me straight
into the old New York of gaslight and police stations I always looked for in the lower city. And of a winter afternoon—the time for which I most lovingly remember the El,
for the color of the winter dusk as it fell through those
painted windows, and the beauty of the snow on the
black cars and iron rails and tar roofs we saw somewhere
off Brooklyn Bridge—when the country stove next to the
change booth blazed and blazed as some crusty old woman

with a pince-nez gave out change, and the heavy turn-
stiles crashed with a roar inside the wooden shed—then,
among the darkly huddled crowds waiting to go out to
the train, looking out on Brooklyn Bridge all dark sweeping cable lines under drifts of snow, I pretended those
were gaslights I saw in the streets below, that all old New
Yorkers were my fathers, and that the train we waited
for could finally take me back—back and back to that old
New York of wood and brownstones and iron, where
Theodore Roosevelt as Police Commissioner had walked
every night.

Beyond was anything old and American—the name
Fraunces Tavern repeated to us on a school excursion; the
eighteenth-century muskets and glazed oil paintings on
the wall; the very streets, the deeper you got into Brooklyn, named after generals of the Revolutionary War—Putnam, Gates, Kosciusko, DeKalb, Lafayette, Pulaski. *Beyond* was the sound of *Desbrosses* Street that steaming
July morning we crossed back on a Jersey ferry, and the
smell of the salt air in the rotting planks floating on the
green scummy waters of the Hudson. *Beyond* was the
watery floor of the Aquarium that smelled of the eternally
wet skins of the seals in the great tank; the curve of lower
Broadway around Bowling Green Park when you went
up to Wall Street; the yellow wicker seats facing each
other in the middle of the El car; the dome of the Manhattan Savings Bank over Chinatown at the entrance to
Manhattan Bridge, and then in Brooklyn again, after we
had traveled from light into dark, dark into light, along
the shuddering shadowy criss-cross of the bridge's pillars,
the miles and miles of Gentile cemeteries where crosses

toppled up and down endless slopes. *Beyond* was that autumn morning in New Haven when I walked up and down two *red* broken paving stones, smelled the leaves burning in the yard, and played with black battered poker chips near the country stove in an aunt's kitchen; it was the speckles on the bananas hanging in the window of the grocery store another aunt owned in the Negro streets just behind Union Station in Washington; the outrageously warm taste of milk fresh from a cow that summer my mother cooked with a dozen others in the same Catskill boarding house; it was the open trolley cars going to Coney Island, the conductor swinging from bar to bar as he came around the ledge collecting fares; it was the *Robert Fulton* going up the Hudson to Indian Point, the ventilators on the upper deck smelling of soup.

Beyond, even in Brownsville, was the summer sound of *flax* when my mother talked of *der heym*. It was the Negroes singing as they passed under our windows late at night on their way back to Livonia Avenue. It was the Children's Library on Stone Avenue, because they had an awning over the front door; in the long peaceful reading room there were storybook tiles over the fireplace and covered deep wooden benches on each side of it where I read my way year after year from every story of King Alfred the Great to *Twenty Thousand Leagues Under the Sea. Beyond* was the burly Jewish truckers from the wholesale fruit markets on Osborne Street sitting in their dark smoky "Odessa" and "Roumanian" tearooms, where each table had its own teapot, and where the men sat over mounds of saucers smoking Turkish cigarettes and beating time to the balalaíka. *Beyond* was the way to the other end of Sutter Avenue, past a store I often went into to buy buttons and thread for my mother, and where the light simmered on the thin upturned curves of the pearl buttons in the window. *Beyond* was the roar in the Pennsylvania freight yards on the way to East New York; even the snow houses we built in the back-yard of a cousin's house on Herzl Street waiting to ambush those thieves from Bristol Street. It was the knife grinder's horse and wagon when he stopped on our block, and an "American" voice called up to every window, *Sharpen knives! Sharpen knives!*—that man had obviously come from a long way off.

Beyond! Beyond! It was the clean, general store smell of packaged white bread in the A&P that Passover week I could not eat matzoh, and going home, hid the soft squunchy loaf of Ward's bread under my coat so that the neighbors would not see. It was the way past the car barns at the end of Rockaway Avenue, that week my father was painting in New Lots, and I took that route for the first time, bringing him his lunch one summer afternoon. I could not wait to get out on the other side of the dark subway station. I had never seen another part of Brownsville where the going was so strange, where streets looked so empty, where the sun felt so hot. It was as if there were not enough houses there to stand in its way. When the sun fell across the great white pile of the new Telephone Company building, you could smell the stucco burning as you passed; then some liquid sweetness that came to me from deep in the rings of freshly cut lumber

stacked in the yards, and the fresh plaster and paint on the
brand-new storefronts. Rawness, sunshiny rawness down
the end streets of the city, as I thought of them then—the
hot ash-laden stink of the refuse dumps in my nostrils
and the only sound at noon the resonant metal plunk of
a tin can I kicked ahead of me as I went my way. Then
two blocks more, and the car barns I loved. The light
falling down the hollows in the corrugated tin roof seemed
to say *Go over! Go over!*, marked the place from which
the stacked trolley cars began all over again their long
weary march into the city. I liked to see them stacked
against each other, a thin trail of track leading out of the
sheds, then another track, then another, until everywhere
you could see, the streets were wild with car tracks pointing the way back to the city.

Beyond was that day they took us first to the Botanic
Garden next to the Brooklyn Museum, and after we went
through the bamboo gate into the Japanese Garden,
crossed over a curved wooden bridge past the stone figure
of a heron dreaming in the water, I lay in the grass waiting to eat my lunch out of the shoe box and wondered
why water lilies floated half-submerged in the pond and
did not sink. They led us into the museum that day, up
the big stone steps they had then, through vast empty
halls that stung my nose with the prickly smell of new
varnish and were lined with the effigies of medieval Japanese warriors—the black stringy hairs on their wigs oppressively unreal, the faces mock-terrible as they glared
down at us through their stiffly raised swords, everything
in that museum wearisome and empty and smelling of
floor polish until they pushed us through a circular room

upstairs violently ablaze with John Singer Sargent's water-
colors of the Caribbean and into a long room lined with
oily dim farmscapes of America in the nineteenth century, and I knew I would come back, that I would have
to come back.

Museums and parks were related, both oases to stop in
"beyond." But in some way museums and parks were painful, each an explosion of unbearable fullness in my brain.
I could never go home from the Brooklyn Museum, a
walk around the reservoir in Central Park, or sit in a
rowboat Sunday afternoons in Prospect Park—where your
voice hallooed against the stone walls of the footbridge as
you waited in that sudden cold darkness below, boat
against boat, to be pushed on to the boathouse and so
end the afternoon—without feeling the same sadness that
came after the movies. The day they took us to the Children's Museum—rain was dripping on the porch of that
old wooden house, the halls were lined with Audubon
prints and were hazel in the thin antique light—I was left
with the distinct impression that I had been stirring between my fingers dried earth and fallen leaves that I had
found in between the red broken paving stones of some
small American town. I seemed to see neighborhood rocks
and minerals in the dusty light of the late afternoon slowly
stirring behind glass at the back of the village museum.
But that same day they took us to Forest Park in Queens,
and I saw a clearing filled with stone picnic tables—
nothing had ever cried out such a welcome as those stone
tables in the clearing—saw the trees in their dim green
recede in one long moving tide back into dusk, and gasped

in pain when the evening rushed upon us before I had a chance to walk that woodland through.

There was never enough time. The morning they led us through the Natural History Museum, under the skeletons of great whales floating dreamlike on wires from the ceiling, I had to wait afterward against the meteor in the entrance yard for my dizziness to pass. Those whales! those whales! But that same morning they took us across Central Park to the Metropolitan, and entering through the back door in from the park, I was flung spinning in a bewilderment of delight from the Greek discus-throwers to the Egyptians to the long rows of medieval knights to the breasts of Venus glistening in my eyes as she sat—some curtain drawn before her hiding the worst of her nakedness—smiling with Mars and surrounded by their children.

The bewilderment eased, a little, when we went up many white steps directly to the American paintings. There was a long, narrow, corridor-looking room lined with the portraits of seventeenth-century merchants and divines—nothing for me there as they coldly stared at me, their faces uninterruptedly rosy in time. But far in the back, in an alcove near the freight elevator, hung so low and the figures so dim in the faint light that I crouched to take them in, were pictures of New York some time after the Civil War—skaters in Central Park, a red muffler flying in the wind; a gay crowd moving round and round Union Square Park; horse cars charging between the brownstones of lower Fifth Avenue at dusk. I could not believe my eyes. Room on room they had painted my city, my country—Winslow Homer's dark oblong of

Union soldiers making camp in the rain, tenting tonight, tenting on the old camp ground as I had never thought I *would* get to see them when we sang that song in school; Thomas Eakins's solitary sculler on the Schuylkill, resting to have his picture taken in the yellow light bright with patches of some raw spring in Pennsylvania showing on the other side of him; and most wonderful to me then, John Sloan's picture of a young girl standing in the wind on the deck of a New York ferryboat—surely to Staten Island, and just about the year of my birth?—looking out to water.

It had to be something dark, oily, glazed, faintly flaring into gaslight at dusk. Dusk in America any time after the Civil War would be the corridor back and back into that old New York under my feet that always left me half-stunned with its audible cries for recognition. The American past was gaslight and oil glaze, the figures painted dark and growing darker each year on the back walls of the Metropolitan. But they had some strange power over my mind as we went down the white steps into Fifth Avenue at the closing bell—the little Greek heralds on top of the traffic boxes gravely waving me on, my own loneliness gleaming back at me as the street lamps shone on their nude gold chests—that would haunt me any time I ever walked down Fifth Avenue again in the first early evening light.

It would have to be dusk. Sitting on the fire escape warm spring afternoons over the Oliver Optics, I read them over and over because there was something about old New York in them—often the dimmest drawing in the ad on the back cover of a newsboy howling his papers as he walked past the *World* building in the snow—that brought back that day at the Metropolitan. I saw Park Row of a winter afternoon in the 1880's, the snow falling into the dark stone streets under Brooklyn Bridge, newsboys running under the maze of telegraph wires that darkened every street of the lower city. How those wires haunted me in every photograph I found of old New York—indescribably heavy, they sagged between the poles; the very streets seemed to sink under their weight. The past was that forest of wires hung over lower New York at five o'clock—dark, heavy, dark; of the time, surely, my parents had first stepped out on the shores of New York at Castle Garden; of the time they had built all police stations in? Walking past our police station on East New York Avenue, I would always be stopped in my tracks by an abysmal nostalgia for the city as it had once been. The green lamps on each side of the station, the drifters along the steps that led down into the public urinals, even the wire netting in the doors of the patrol wagons whose terrifying backs squatted side by side in the yard—all plunged me so suddenly into my daylight dream of walking New York streets in the 1880's that I would wait on the corner, holding my breath, perfectly sure that my increasingly dim but still almighty Police Commissioner Theodore Roosevelt would come down the steps at any moment.

It would have to be dusk in the lower city. That steaming spring afternoon I was on my way to a lesson at the Music School Settlement, and deep in Bleecker Street could see the streaky whitewashed letters on the back

walls of the tenements FLETCHER'S CASTORIA CHILDREN
CRY FOR IT CHARLES S. FLETCH . . . , there was a sickening sweetness out of the fur shops, and I saw for the
first time derelicts sleeping across the cellar doors—some
with empty pint bottles behind their heads; some with
dried blood and spittle on their cracked lips, as if they
had scraped themselves with knives; some with their flies
open, so that the storekeepers cooling themselves in the
doorways grinned with scorn and disgust. I knew those
men as strangers left over from another period, waiting
for me to recognize them. The old pea jackets and caps
they slept in were somehow not of the present; they were
still in the work clothes they wore on the last job they had
had; they bore even in their faces the New York of another century, and once I followed one up the Bowery,
strangely sure that he would lead me back into my own,
lost, old New York. The El over my head thundered just
as it did in that early New York of the Oliver Optics;
there were signs hung above the roofs, gold letters on a
black field, advertising jewelry, Klein's Special Size Suits
For Fat Men, pawnshops. Dusty particles of daylight fell
between the tracks of the El; I had never seen anything
so right; it was dusk, dusk everywhere in the lower city
now all the way to Cooper Square and Bible House and
Astor Place, where even the books and prints and sheet
music on the stalls were dusty old, and as I went up the
black stairs of the El station with the Gold Stripe silk
stocking ad teasing my eye from step to step, only the
cries of the old Jewish women selling salted pretzels near
Union Square broke the spell.

But why that long ride home at all? Why did they live

there and we always in "Brunzvil"? Why were they *there*, and we always *here?* Why was it always *them* and *us*, Gentiles and us, *alrightniks* and us? Beyond Brownsville was all "the city," that other land I could see for a day, but with every next day back on the block, back to the great wall behind the drugstore I relentlessly had to pound with a handball. Beyond was the strange world of Gentiles, all of them with flaxen hair, who hated Jews, especially poor Jews, had ugly names for us I could never read or hear without seeing Pilsudski's knife cold against our throats. To be a Jew meant that one's very right to existence was always being brought into question. Everyone knew this—even the Communists summer nights on Pitkin Avenue said so, could make the most listless crowd weep with reminders of what they were doing to us in Fascist Poland, Roumania, Hungary. It was what I had always heard in the great *Kol Nidre* sung in the first evening hours of the Day of Atonement, had played on my violin for them Friday evenings in the dining room whenever I felt lost and wanted to show them how much I loved them, knew them through and through, would suffer loyally with them. Jews were Jews; Gentiles were Gentiles. The line between them had been drawn for all time. What had my private walks into the city to do with anything!

But one humid morning, that summer I was confirmed at thirteen, I wearily unwound the stiff black thongs of the phylacteries from my left arm, which is nearest the heart; removed from my forehead, for that is over the brain, the little black box in which is inscribed the *Hear O Israel, the Lord Our God, the Lord is One;* folded and put away the silk blue-striped prayer shawl I loved—and wearily climbed out onto the fire escape, into the steaming midmorning air, absently holding my prayer book. I had never really looked at that lefthand English page of the prayer book, had imagined from something even my parents had said, perplexed and amused as they were by my private orthodoxy, that it was not entirely proper to look at prayers in English translation. But early summer morning in Brownsville: the pigeons rasping in their cages, the kids still too young for handball with a regulation black hard ball already at their first game of boxball in the street, the sun so fierce on the iron floor of the fire escape that I had to sit on the windowsill, my bottom prickly on the pebbled stone. Everything in sight looked half-dead; I could see some women already out on their kitchen chairs for the day, panting as the sweat ran down their red angry necks into the unbuttoned tops of their housedresses. I listlessly picked up my little prayer book, too tired now even to finish reading the last blessings, and in an agony of surprise, as if I could distinctly hear great seas breaking around me, read aloud to myself:

For the Lord is a Great God, and a great king above all gods. In his hand are the depths of the earth; and the summit of the hills is his also. The sea is his, for he made it; and his hands formed the dry land. Come, let us bow down, bend the knee, and prostrate ourselves before the Lord who has made us. For he is our God, and we are the flock of his pasture, and the sheep of his herd; even this day if ye will hearken to his voice. Harden not your hearts, as in the day of strife and temptation in the wilder-

*ness, when your fathers provoked me, and proved me,
though they saw my wondrous work. Forty years was I
grieved with this generation, and said, it is a people of err-
ing heart, for they have not considered my ways. Then I
swore in my wrath that they should not come to the place
of my rest.*

*True and certain, established, sure, just, faithful, be-
loved, esteemed, desirable and pleasant, awful, mighty,
regular, acceptable, good and beautiful, is this word unto
us for evermore.*

I had never realized that this, this *deepness,* lay under
the gloomy obscurities of *Shabbes* in our little wooden
synagogue on Chester Street; that my miserable *melamed*
with a few dried peas sticking to his underlip and ready
to slap my hands at every mistake had known *this. When
your fathers provoked me!* How many fathers I had!
Morning after morning now, the phylacteries forgotten,
I sat on the fire escape with the Hebrew Bible whose left
pages in English I had looked into only to enlist the
support of Deborah, fiery prophetess of Israel, and now
glowed when I came to those lines in the Book of Ruth
that seemed to speak for me to the Jews: *Urge me not
to leave thee, to return from following thee; for whither
thou goest, will I go; and where thou lodgest, will I lodge;
thy people shall be my people, and thy God my God.*
How many fathers! How, *even as* the elders smelling of
snuff in our little wooden synagogue at evening service
—how each of my fathers must have stood up alone, and
each wrapped round and round in his prayer shawl, as at
the moment of his death, addressed himself in the deepest

prayer to God alone. We were a mighty people, a mighty people, and He our mighty father. I could feel in the surge of that prayer book the divine power of that Great One before Whom I had bound my left arm in the black thongs of the phylacteries and had strapped the little black box on my forehead, thus pledging my heart and my brain in devotion to Him. It was all One, I read now: from the power of the All-Highest to the lowliest Jew in prayer, it was all One. Now, on the "Great Day," the Atonement Day itself, I could wait patiently through the long morning and endless afternoon of fasting and prayer for that unforgettable moment when the faithful bowed their heads, and, each man smiting himself on the breast over and over in the bitterest repentance for every sin committed during the year, all went through the long catalogue in unison, finding in its enumeration, as I thought, a kind of purifying ecstasy, for they were summing up the whole earthly life of Brownsville:

> *Our God, and God of Our Fathers,*
> *Verily, we confess, we have sinned*
>
> *We have trespassed*
> *We have dealt treacherously*
> *We have stolen*
> *We have spoken slander*
> *We have committed iniquity*
>   *and have done wickedly*
> *We have acted presumptuously*
> *We have committed violence*
> *We have said falsehood*
> *We have counseled evil*

We have uttered lies
We have scorned
We have rebelled
We have blasphemed
We have revolted
We have acted perversely
We have transgressed

The voice that spoke in that prayer book seemed to
come out of my very bowels. There was something grand
and austere in it that confirmed everything I had felt in
my bones about being a Jew: the fierce awareness of life
to the depths, every day and in every hour: the commit-
ment: the hunger.

Only, there was no gladness in it. Morning after morning, as I read that prayer book on the fire escape, the
English words, too, though so strangely fundamental that
it moved me just to say them aloud, took on the same
abasement before the monotonous God I had always
known. There was a familiar dread in that prayer book,
a despairing supplication, that reminded me of my mother's
humility before the doctors in the public dispensary on
Thatford Avenue and of my own fear of all teachers at
school. It looked as if Brownsville, too, had been set up
by divine order. Was being a Jew the same as living in
Brownsville? Were they really Jews, those who lived beyond Brownsville? I wanted nothing so much as to be a
"good Jew," as they said in the Talmud Torah on Stone
Avenue. But even in their great synagogue, under the
chandeliers terrible with sun all through the "Great Day"
of Atonement, I had heard them up in the front pews

nearest the Ark making a little deal whenever they looked up at intervals from the prayers they were mumbling so fast that even they, I guessed, had no notion what the words meant. They neither believed nor disbelieved; they never thought about it; He had been with us a long time. Only, there was no promise of gladness in Him. Surely He had been real in *der heym?* I had read about the Chassidim, "great enthusiasts, dancers, walkers"—poor East European Jews, only the poorest, but so full of the Lord that they danced before Him in their joy. There were my people! But when you asked around, hoping there had been at least one Chassid somewhere among all your many praying grandfathers and great grandfathers and great-great-grandfathers—surely there had been at least one! surely there was one still among those ancient bearded elders in our synagogue!—they shrugged their shoulders, said something about old-fashioned customs, *mishegóyim,* crazy ones, comfortably took another pinch of snuff, first in one nostril, then in the other, sneezed heartily, and went back to their prayers.

So if you had sat too long on the fire escape, were getting dizzy and lonely in the sun with all your own thoughts locked up inside you—you had only to shake a leg, take up a book to read on the long subway ride, and getting off anywhere, walk it off—not ashamed to think your own thoughts, to sing, ready to meet beautiful unmet Chassidim, even to pray as you pleased. Walking, I always knew how I felt by the music in my head.

Now, summer by summer, when I went about Brooklyn delivering the *Eagle;* or went up and down the sands of Coney Island selling Eskimo Pies; or stopped in the

Brooklyn Museum to look at the Ryders; or in front of the Library at Fifth and 42nd, waiting for the light to change, laughed right out loud because I had just sat my first exultant hour in those long sun-filled reading rooms on the third floor; or floundered and gawked my way past Cleopatra's Needle to the back door of the Metropolitan, to take in, now, Winslow Homer's *The Gulf Stream* and Thomas Eakins's portrait of Walt Whitman in a lace collar; or with a knapsack my mother had made for me out of old laundry bags walked over the Palisades to Alpine—now, when I stopped to catch my breath under the shepherd's crook of a lamp pole in Brooklyn, the streets themselves reeled for joy, and whenever I humbly retired into the subway for the long ride home, something would automatically pull me out at Brooklyn Bridge for one last good walk across the promenade before I fell into the subway again.

For all those first summer walks into the city, all daily walks across the bridge for years afterward, when I came to leave Brownsville at last, were efforts to understand one single half-hour at dusk, on a dark winter day, the year I was fourteen. There had been some school excursion that day to City Hall and the courts of lower New York, and looking up at the green dome of the *World* as we came into Park Row, I found myself separated from the class, and decided to go it across the bridge alone. I remember holding a little red volume of THE WORLD'S GREATEST SELECTED SHORT STORIES in my hand as I started out under the groined arcade of the Municipal Building and the rusty green-black terminal of the El sweeping onto the bridge from Park Row—somewhere in the course of that walk across the bridge the last of those volumes got lost for all time. Evening was coming on fast, great crowds in thick black overcoats were pounding up the staircases to the El; the whole bridge seemed to shake under the furious blows of that crowd starting for home.

Rush hour above, on every side, below: the iron wheels of the El trains shooting blue-white sparks against the black, black tracks sweeping in from Chinatown and Oliver Street under the black tar roofs and fire escapes and empty window boxes along the grimy black tenements on whose sides I could see the streaky whitewashed letters CHILDREN CRY FOR IT FLETCHER'S CASTORIA CHARLES S. FLETCHER; trolley cars bounding up into the air on each side of me, their bells clanging, clanging; cars sweeping off the bridge and onto the bridge in the narrow last roadways before me.

Then a long line of naked electric bulbs hung on wires above the newsstands and hot dog stands in the arcade, raw light glittering above the flaky iron rust, newsboys selling the *Evening World*, the smell of popcorn and of frankfurters sizzling on the grill. And now up a flight of metal-edged wooden steps and into the open at last, the evening coming on faster and faster, a first few flakes of snow in the air, the lights blue and hard up one side of the transparent staircases in Wall Street, dark on another; the river black, inky black; then the long hollow boom shivering the worn wooden planks under my feet as a ship passes under the bridge.

Dusk of a dark winter's day that first hour walking

Brooklyn Bridge. Suddenly I felt lost and happy as I went up another flight of steps, passed under the arches of the tower, and waited, next to a black barrel, at the railing of the observation platform. The trolleys clanged and clanged; every angry stalled car below sounded its horn as, bumper to bumper, they all poked their way along the bridge; the El trains crackled and thundered over my right shoulder. A clock across the street showed its lighted face; along the fire escapes of the building were sculptured figures of runners and baseball players, of prize fighters flexing their muscles and wearing their championship belts, just as they did in the *Police Gazette*. But from that platform under the tower the way ahead was strange. Only the electric sign of the Jewish Daily *Forward*, burning high over the tenements of the East Side, suddenly stilled the riot in my heart as I saw the cables leap up to the tower, saw those great meshed triangles leap up and up, higher and still higher—Lord my Lord, when will they cease to drive me up with them in their flight?—and then, each line singing out alone the higher it came and nearer, fly flaming into the topmost eyelets of the tower.

Somewhere below they were roasting coffee, handling spices—the odor was in the pillars, in the battered wooden planks of the promenade under my feet, in the blackness upwelling from the river. A painter's scaffold dangled down one side of the tower over a spattered canvas. Never again would I walk Brooklyn Bridge without smelling that coffee, those spices, the paint on that canvas. The trolley car clanged, clanged, clanged taking me home that day from the bridge. Papa, where are they taking me? Where in this beyond are they taking me?

Every next day the battle with the back wall of the drugstore began again. There was something about that wall just under the front windows of our house that constantly angered me, then blankly receiving every blow, called on me to try again. I mastered that wall every day, but could never know if I had really won. "What have you boys got against that wall?" my mother used to say wonderingly. "What is in a wall?" But at any moment of the afternoon or evening, so long as there was still light to see by, you might see a boy slowly and cagily throwing a ball against it with a sidelong look at you, shaping the strokes off his right arm as if he were sharpening a knife. You had to take him up; his insolence blocked you on every side; he would test you up and down the whole length of that wall. So that when at last you stood up against it in a game *"for money,"* the real thing, between the milk cans in front of the grocery windows and the jagged iron spikes above the stairway to the cellar, and you saw that first high bounding serve floating spinning eerily at you over the telephone wires, your whole heart twisted as you unconsciously leaped up to smash it back, to ignore the square aching pain of that hard rubber ball in the palm of your hand—to send it back, only to send it back!

In that moment everything waited on my performance; the women at their windows seemed to be quiet, watching me. As I faced that wall in the thudding silence, my arm crooked in defiance, it seemed to me I could hear voices two blocks away as I tasted the grime of the cellar steps and the white ooze under the freshly pasted Hecker's Flour sign. Then everything fell scalding into hammer blows. Wiping the sweat off our chins only when we panted back from the wall after each hit, knees bent and hands on our thighs with professional alertness, each body slightly stooped in the agony of effort, we gravely and suspiciously danced around each other, darting into vacated positions with our hands still lifted, ready for anything—then "accidentally" ran in front of our opponents to block their view, and when it was our turn to hit the ball back, rushed in for a killer, sometimes flinging ourselves in our fury against the wall itself. I think now of my astonishment as I rushed at it, the deep spaces between the brick yawning up at me, the tar letters DAZZY DAZZY DAZZY unwinding in my mind as I danced back to the curb. There was a terrible pre-eminence in myself when I stood right up against it, alone before the wall to hit a serve. I could feel myself bowing down the whole length of that wall, waiting to lash out.

I was afraid of the cellar. Each family in the house had a coal bin of its own in the days before steam heat. I would help my father and mother shovel the winter's coal into our bin, then shovel it out again every other day into a black pail that I carried upstairs to our kitchen. You had to fasten the Yale lock good and hard; it was always expected that the tough guys on the block would break into your bin. The cellar was a winter clubhouse.

Whenever I forced open the cellar doors next to the barbershop and let myself down the narrow steps with the pail banging behind me and an inch of candle burning in my hand, I could take in, along with the smell of coal dust and damp and the stray cats mewing in the bins, some wilder, rancid smell that told me someone was "hiding away" with a girl. That cellar was made up in even parts of silence and blackness. Only the clang of the cellar doors as they fell together behind me, or a mound of coal shifting against the bin doors—then the cats screamed in fright—ever broke into the damp blackness of the cellar. But when my candle blew out, and I scraped another kitchen match against the floor, I thought I could hear something stirring near the fuse boxes. Then the dripping tallow thickened wildly on my thumb and the acrid sulphur smell of the match burned at my nostrils. Something was happening. Someone was there. But door after door the bins looked blind and shut. From the coal bins to the backyard there was nothing but damp black passage—only a faint haze of blue smoke under the fuse boxes. Where did they do it? How? Once, as the bin door creaked too loudly as I opened the lock, and my shovel scraped against the floor, I thought I heard footsteps running toward the yard.

The yard smelled of brick and was thickmatted with clotheslines. On every side the white backs of the two tenements rose up around you, enclosing you in a narrow circle littered with splintered crates, loose sheets of old newspaper, garbage cans, and the thin green ooze left behind by the cats. Great shafts of light poured through the space between the roofs, rewhitening the sheets hung

across the yard. Every particle of light falling into the
yard seemed to dissolve into the color of that dusty white
brick at the back, revolved in the air as if shot out of a
great open bag of flour. When you were in the yard, you
could look only straight up, the clotheslines seemed about
to strangle you—the place was so narrow, so narrow; held
you in a cylinder of white dust and the noise from the
back windows.

Every voice raised in that yard crashed against the walls
like a bullet. One by one they would come there all
through the first warm afternoons of spring—the Yiddish
tenors, the old clothes men, the forgotten fiddlers, the
German cornetists, even Blumka the madwoman, who
would drag her cart in if the women on the block had
not given her enough, and howl curses up at the back windows—one by one each would stand up on that little slope
where we raised snowhouses in winter, and alone in the
yard, cry up to the housewives who were wrapping pennies
in little pieces of newspaper before throwing them into
the yard. The singers always sang the same story, always
cried to the same grief. But it was not for their music I
listened—it was to the voice itself rebounding against brick;
the voice that crept up each window to the roof, insinu-
ated itself into every back bedroom and down the hollows
in a woman's back as standing against the window, she
raised her hands to pull a dress over her head—a voice
struggling to be heard against the pandemonium that filled
the yard, that was sometimes entirely lost in the swish of
the sheets and the clatter of the pulleys as the clotheslines were brought in, but always bounding up again hard
and clear in the great narrow shaft, forced me to look

through the tangled web of clotheslines to the figure standing alone in the middle of the yard.

From the bottom of that yard sensations reached me for which I would have no final accounting. They stole up at me from the grittiness of the brick in the staleness of the long afternoons, the mewing of the cats in the cellar, the orange rinds and newspapers and splintered wooden crates, until I could feel what I thought like a new layer over my skin. Those singers had something to tell me, simply by the way they held the depths of the bottom of the yard. Sometimes the voice had to fight every sound from the back windows; when I looked down, I had a sudden image of the singer at the bottom of a well, sinking under the weight of the clotheslines, but in one last furious entreaty to be heard, still pitting himself against every scream and cry falling into the yard. But below the easy Yiddish plaint, the dry sobs and tears, the stolid singsong *I cash old clóthes! I cash old clóthes!*, I heard some smiling indifference that lisped across the yard drop by drop, reached up to a woman's shoulders naked at the window like a negligent caress.

The fruit and vegetable stand, the drygoods store, the luggage shop, the rummage shop that sold second-hand books. Only the corsetmaker's is left, his windows still lined with his old European diplomas and gold-sealed certificates of honor presented to him in 1906 at the Brussels Fair. Everywhere else—BARGAINS BARGAINS—the second-hand furniture stores have taken over our block, turning the old life out into the street. But walking past what had once been the candy store, I tasted all the old sweetness of malted milks on my tongue, breathed again the strong sweet fumes of the Murads and Helmars and Lord Salisburys our fathers smoked. Going past what had once been the rummage shop I could feel in my pocket the touch of all the hand-me-down Frank and Dick Merriwells I had bought there for a nickel each, and the copy of Edward Dowden's life of Browning I had read because it cost a dime, and the muddy paper-backed edition of *Great Poems in the English Language* where I first read Blake:

> Little Lamb, I'll tell thee,
> Little Lamb, I'll tell thee:

It is the old drugstore on the corner I miss most. All those maple beds in the window have made that store stupid; it has nothing to say to me now. Once it was the most exciting threshold I had ever crossed. In the windows glass urns of rose and pink and blue colored water hung from chains; in the doorway I took in the smell of camphor and mothballs and brown paper wardrobes whenever I earned three cents calling someone to the telephone; across from the telephone booths there hung over the black stippled wallpaper that large color picture, a present from a dye company, of General Israel Putnam on his horse riding up some stone steps just ahead of the British, but with his face turned back to me so that I could see it glorious with defiance.

Night after night in the winter, long after I had thrown my book on the kitchen floor and had pulled the string of the bulb in the ceiling, I would push myself as deep under the quilt as I could get, and lie there on the kitchen chairs near the stove thinking of Mrs. Solovey. And often in the middle of the night, I would be awakened by the sound of Negroes singing as they passed under our windows on their way back to Livonia Avenue, and would pick up my book again as if to follow out to the end the phrase I had just heard. Then I seemed to confuse her blond hair with the long hair shining down the backs of the women in the placards on Mr. Solovey's counter advertising brilliantine. In those placards, their eyes wide open in adoration of their own richness, all women looked as if they were dreaming, too. Sometimes they had the hair of Blumka the madwoman, and sometimes the look of our unmarried cousin in her embroidered Russian blouse, long after she had gone away from us forever and I would sit on her bed staring miserably at the bookcase.

Under the quilt at night, I could dream even before I went to sleep. Yet even there I could never see Mrs. Solovey's face clearly, but still ran round and round the block looking for her after I had passed her kitchen window. It was an old trick, the surest way of getting to sleep: I put the quilt high over my head and lay there burrowing as deep into the darkness as I could get, thinking of her through the long black hair the women on the counter wore. Then I would make up dreams before going to sleep: a face behind the lattice of a summer house, half-hidden in thick green leaves; the hard dots sticking out of the black wallpaper below; the day my mother was ill and our cousin had taken me to school. The moment I felt myself drifting into sleep, my right knee jerked as if I had just caught myself from tripping over something in the gutter. Then I would start up in fright, and perfectly awake, watching the flames dance out from under the covers in the stove, would dream of the druggist's wife and of her blond hair. I had not seen many fair-haired people until I met Mrs. Solovey. There were the Polish "broads" from East New York, smoking cigarettes on someone's lap in the "Coney Island" dives across the street from school, the sheen down their calves and the wickedness of their painted lips what you expected of a blonde. There were the four daughters of our Russian Christian janitor, Mrs. Krylot, all of them with bright golden hair and faces deeply carved and immobile as a wood cut. But they did not count; they smelled of the salt butter the Gentiles used; their blondness seemed naive and uncouth. Mrs. Solovey's I had identified from the first with something direct and sinful.

The Soloveys had been very puzzling; from the day they had come to our tenement, taking over the small dark apartment on the ground floor next to his drugstore, no one had been able to make them out at all. Both the Soloveys had had an inaccessible air of culture that to the end had made them seem visitors among us. They had brought into our house and street the breath of another world, where parents read books, discussed ideas at the table, and displayed a quaint, cold politeness addressing each other. The Soloveys had traveled; they had lived in Palestine, France, Italy. They were "professional" people, "enlightened"—she, it was rumored, had even been a physician or "some kind of scientist," we could never discover which.

The greatest mystery was why they had come to live in Brownsville. We looked down on them for this, and suspected them. To come *deliberately* to Brownsville, after you had lived in France and Italy! It suggested some moral sickness, apathy, a perversion of all right feelings. The apathy alone had been enough to excite me. They were different!

Of course the Soloveys were extremely poor—how else could they even have thought of moving in among us? There were two drab little girls with Hebrew names, who went about in foreign clothes, looking so ill-nourished that my mother was indignant, and vowed to abduct them from their strange parents for an afternoon and feed them up thoroughly. Mrs. Solovey was herself so thin, shy, and gently aloof that she seemed to float away from me whenever I passed her in the hall. There was no doubt in our minds that the Soloveys had come to Brownsville at the end of their road. But what had they hoped to gain from us? If they had ever thought of making money in a Brownsville drugstore, they were soon disenchanted. The women on the block bought such drugs as they had to when illness came. But they did not go in for luxuries, and they had a hearty, familiar way of expecting credit as their natural right from a neighbor and fellow Jew that invariably made Mr. Solovey furious. That was only for the principle of the thing: he showed no interest in making money. He seemed to despise his profession, and the store soon became so clogged with dust and mothballs and camphor-smelling paper wardrobes and the shampoo ads indignantly left him by salesmen of beauty preparations which he refused to stock, that people hated to go in. They all thought him cynical and arrogant. Although he understood well enough when someone addressed him in Yiddish, he seemed to dislike the language, and only frowned, curtly nodding his head to show that he understood. The Soloveys talked Russian to each other, and though we were impressed to hear them going on this way between themselves, everyone else disliked them for it. Not to use our familiar neighborhood speech, not even the English expected of the "educated," meant that they wanted us not to understand them.

Mr. Solovey was always abrupt and ill-tempered, and when he spoke at all, it was to throw a few words out from under his walrus mustache with an air of bitter disdain for us all. His whole manner as he stood behind his counter seemed to say: "I am here because I am here, and I may talk to you if I have to! Don't expect me to enjoy it!" His business declined steadily. Everyone else on the block was a little afraid of him, for he would look through a prescription with such surly impatience that rumors spread he was a careless and inefficient pharmacist, and probably unsafe to use. If he minded, he never showed it. There was always an open book on the counter, usually a Russian novel or a work of philosophy; he spent most of his time reading. He would sit in a greasy old wicker armchair beside the telephone booths, smoking Murads in a brown-stained celluloid holder and muttering to himself as he read. He took as little trouble to keep himself clean as he did his store, and his long drooping mustache and black alpaca coat were always gray with cigarette ash. It looked as if he hated to be roused from his reading even to make a sale, for the slightest complaint sent him into a rage. "I'll never come back to you, Mr. Solovey!" someone would threaten. "Thanks be to God!" he would shout back. "Thanks God! Thanks God! It will be a great pleasure not to see you!" "A *meshúgener*," the women on the block muttered to each other. "A real crazy one. Crazy to death."

The Soloveys had chosen to live in Brownsville when they could have lived elsewhere, and this made them mysterious. Through some unfathomable act of will, they had chosen us. But for me they were beyond all our endless gossip and speculation about them. They fascinated me simply because they were so different. There was some open madness in the Soloveys' relation to each other for which I could find no parallel, not even a clue, in the lives of our own parents. Whenever I saw the strange couple together, the gold wedding ring on his left hand thick as hers, I felt they were still lovers. Yet the Soloveys were not rich. They were poor as we were, even poorer. I had never known anyone like them. They were weary people, strange and bereft people. I felt they had floated into Brownsville like wreckage off the ship of foreignness and "culture" and the great world outside. And there was that visible tie between them, that wedding ring even a man could wear, some deep consciousness of each other, that excited me, it seemed so illicit. And this was all the more remarkable because, though lovers, they were so obviously unhappy lovers. Had they chucked each other on the chin, had they kissed in public, they would have seemed merely idiotic. No, they seemed to hate each other, and could often be heard quarreling in their apartment, which sent every sound out into the hallway and the street. These quarrels were not like the ones we heard at home. There were no imprecations, no screams, no theatrical sobs: "You're killing me! You're plunging the knife straight into my heart! You're putting me into an early grave! May you sink ten fathoms into the earth!" Such bitter accusations were heard among us all the time, but did not mean even that someone disliked you. In Yiddish we broke all the windows to let a little air into the house.

But in the Soloveys' quarrels there was something worse than anger; it was hopelessness. I felt such despair in them, such a fantastic need to confront each other alone all day long, that they puzzled me by not sharing their feelings with their children. *They* alone, the gruff ne'er-do-well husband and his elusive wife, were the family. Their two little girls did not seem to count at all; the lovers, though their love had been spent, still lived only for each other. And it was this that emphasized their strangeness for me —it was as strange as Mr. Solovey's books, as a Brownsville couple speaking Russian to each other, as strange as Mrs. Solovey's delightfully shocking blondness and the unfathomable despair that had brought them to us. In this severe dependence on each other for everything, there was a defiance of the family principle, of us, of their own poverty and apathy, that encouraged me to despise our values as crude and provincial. Only in movies and in *The Sheik* did people abandon the world for love, give themselves up to it—gladly. Yet there was nothing obviously immoral in the conduct of the Soloveys, nothing we could easily describe and condemn. It was merely that they were sufficient to each other; in their disappointment as in their love they were always alone. They left us out, they left Brownsville out; we were nothing to them. In the love despair of the Soloveys something seemed to say that our constant fight "to make sure" was childish, that we looked at life too narrowly, and that in any event, we did not count. Their loneliness went deeper than our solidarity.

And so I loved them. By now I, too, wanted to defy Brownsville. I did not know where or how to begin. I knew only that I could dream all day long while pretending to be in the world, and that my mind was full of visions as intimate with me as loneliness. I felt I was alone, that there were things I had to endure out of loyalty but could never accept, and that whenever I liked, I could swim out from the Brownsville shore to that calm and sunlit sea beyond where *great friends* came up from the deep. Every book I read re-stocked my mind with those great friends who lived out of Brownsville. They came into my life proud and compassionate, recognizing me by a secret sign, whispering through subterranean channels of sympathy: "Alfred! Old boy! What have they done to you!" Walking about, I learned so well to live with them that I could not always tell whether it was they or I thinking in me. As each fresh excitement faded, I felt myself being flung down from great peaks. Sometimes I was not sure which character I was on my walks, there were so many in my head at once; or how I could explain one to the other; but after an afternoon's reading in the "adults'" library on Glenmore Avenue, I would walk past the pushcarts on Belmont Avenue and the market women crying "Oh you darlings! Oh you pretty ones! Come! Come! Eat us alive! Storm us! De-

vour us! Tear us apart!"—proud and alien as Othello, or
dragging my clubfoot after me like the hero of *Of Human
Bondage,* a book I had read to tatters in my amazement
that Mr. W. Somerset Maugham knew me so well. In
that daily walk from Glenmore to Pitkin to Belmont to
Sutter I usually played out the life cycles of at least five
imaginary characters. They did not stay in my mind very
long, for I discovered new books every day; somewhere
I felt them to be unreal, cut off by the sickening clean
edge of the curb; but while they lived, they gave me a
happiness that reverberated in my mind long after I had
reached our street and had turned on the first worn step
of our stoop for one last proud annihilating glance back
at the block.

The Soloveys came into my life as the nearest of all the
great friends. Everything which made them seem queer
on the block deepened their beauty for me. I yearned to
spend the deepest part of myself on someone close, someone I could endow directly with the radiant life of the
brotherhood I joined in books. Passionately attached as I
was to my parents, it had never occurred to me to ask
myself what I thought of them as individuals. They were
the head of the great body to which I had been joined at
birth. There was nothing I could *give* them. I wanted
some voluntary and delighted gift of emotion to rise up
in me; something that would surprise me in the giving,
that would flame directly out of me; that was not, like
the obedience of our family love, a routine affair of every
day. I wanted to bestow love that came from an idea.
All day long in our kitchen my mother and I loved each
other in measures of tribulation well-worn as the *Kol*

Nidre. We looked to each other for support; we recognized each other with a mutual sympathy and irritation; each of us bore some part of the other like a guarantee that the other would never die. I stammered, she used to say, because she stammered; when she was happy, the air on the block tasted new. I could never really take it in that there had been a time, even in *der heym*, when she had been simply a woman alone, with a life in which I had no part.

Running around the block summer evenings, I always stopped in front of the Soloveys' windows and looked across the spiked iron fence above the cellar steps on the chance that I might see Mrs. Solovey moving around her kitchen. I still spent hours every afternoon hanging around the telephone; he simply refused to answer it; and sometimes I would sit in his greasy old wicker armchair outside the booths, excitedly taking in the large color picture of General Israel Putnam on his horse riding up the stone steps just ahead of the British, the hard dots that stuck out of the black stippled wallpaper, the ladies dreaming in the brilliantine ads on the counter, the mothballs and camphor and brown paper wardrobes that always smelled of something deep, secret, inside. I liked to watch Mr. Solovey as he sat there reading behind his counter, perfectly indifferent to everyone, glowering and alone, the last wet brown inch of cigarette gripped so firmly between his teeth that I could never understand why the smoke did not get into his eyes or burn the edges of his mustache. It excited me just to watch someone read like that.

But now, night after night as I lay on our kitchen chairs

under the quilt, I found I could will some sudden picture of his wife, hospitable and grave in the darkness. Everything that now made her so lustrous to me—her air of not being quite placed in life, her gentle aloofness, her secret carnality—was missing in her husband's appearance. The store went from bad to worse, and he seemed to plant himself more and more in the back of it like a dead tree defying us to cut him down. He never even looked at me when I sat in his wicker armchair near the telephone booths, but barricaded himself behind his counter, where his Russian novels lay in a mound of dust and gradually displaced the brilliantine ads and the ten-cent toilet articles. Except in emergencies, or when I had someone to call to the telephone, hardly anyone now came into the store. Most people were afraid of him, and the boys on the block took a special delight in exasperating him by banging a handball just above his kitchen windows. Yet there was something indomitable in his bearing, and with it an ill-concealed contempt for us all, that made it impossible to feel sorry for him. His blazing eyes, his dirty alpaca jacket always powdered with a light dust of cigarette ash, the walrus mustache that drooped down the sides of his mouth with such an expression of disgust for us, for his life—everything seemed to say that he did not care how he lived or what we thought of him. Having determined to fail, his whole bearing told me he had chosen *us* to watch him; and he would fail just as he liked, shocking us as he went under, like a man drowning before our eyes whom our cries could not save. Perhaps he liked to shock us; perhaps our shame and incredulity at seeing him put back so far were things he viciously en-

joyed, since the whole manner of his life was an assault
on our own hopes and our plain sense of right and wrong.
There was something positive in him that had chosen to
die, that mocked all our admiration for success. We failed
every day, but we fought our failure; we hated it; we
measured every action by its help in getting us around
failure. Mr. Solovey confused us. In some unspoken way,
full of bitterness and scorn, he seemed to say that success
did not matter.

I alone knew his secret; I, too, was in love with his
wife. I was perfectly sure that all his misery came from
the force and bafflement of his attachment to her. The
hopeless love between them had scoured them clean of
normal concerns, like getting money and "making sure"
and being parents. The store went to pieces, the two little
girls in their foreign clothes played jacks all afternoon
long on the front steps, Mr. Solovey denounced us with
his eyes, and Mrs. Solovey walked among us in her dream
of a better life. But alone, I used to think every time I
passed their door on my way upstairs, they glided up and
down in their apartment like two goldfish in the same
tank. This was the way I saw them; she was the only key
I had to their mystery. I based it entirely on my incredulous delight in her.

It was her dreaminess, her air of not being quite related
to anything around her, that pleased me most. She floated
through our lives; in most ways she was never really with
us. I saw her so seldom that afterward, whenever I sum-
moned up her face a second before dropping off to
sleep, I could never actually tell whether it was her face
I remembered, or the face of another woman with blond

hair who had once lived in our house. Under the quilt,
all women with blond hair and gold wedding rings shining from behind the lattices of a summer house soon took
on the same look as they comfortably placed one hand
over my back, had the same wide-open dreamy smile as
the women in the brilliantine ads on the counter. Only
the name I had invented for Mrs. Solovey could bring
her instantly back to me. I would say it over and over
under my breath, just to hear the foreign syllables ring
out—Elizavéta, Elizavéta, no name they ever gave a good
Jewish woman; Elizavéta, Elizavéta, I was so astonished
to think of Mrs. Solovey, a Jewish woman, speaking Russian every day; Elizavéta, Elizavéta, more accessible than
any character I had ever found in a book, but as pliable;
more real, but as deliciously unreal. There she was, only
two flights of stairs below us, someone I might pass on
the block every day, yet a woman like no other I had ever
seen. Her blondness flashed out in our tenement, among
our somber and dogged faces, with a smiling wantonness.
Die blonde! Die blonde! In her blondness and languor I
seemed to hear the comfortable rustle of nakedness itself.

One day she came into our kitchen, looking for my
mother to make a dress for her. I was alone, doing my
French lesson at the table. When she spoke to me in her
timid, Russian-gruff accent, I felt myself flying back to
Anna Karenina. There was a grandeur of suffering in
her face, in the spindly thinness of her body in the old-
fashioned dress, that immediately sent me to that world I
had heard of all my life. I was glad my mother was out;
I felt I could now enjoy Mrs. Solovey alone. She stood
at the kitchen door smiling uneasily, deliberating with

herself whether to wait, and when I pressed her, timidly sat down on the other side of the table. I had made so much of her that seeing her so close gave me a curious feeling of alarm. How would it turn out? How did you address your shameful secret love when she walked into a kitchen, and sat down with you, and smiled, smiled nervously, never fitting herself to the great design? Looking at her there, I scorned her mean role as a wife and mother, held to the wildly unhappy husband below, to the two little girls who were always playing jacks by themselves on the front steps. She was Anna, Tolstoy's and my Anna, the sensual and kindly and aristocratically aloof heroine who was unhappily married, who bewitched men's minds, who shocked everyone in St. Petersburg by the gentle power that welled up despite her gold wedding ring. She might have just walked in from a frosty afternoon's ride with her lover on the Nevsky Prospekt, swathed in furs, a mink toque on her head, shyly impervious to the stares and whispers of the envious crowd.

"You are perhaps going to school, young man?" Mrs. Solovey asked after a long silence.

I nodded.

"Do you, uh, do you like the going to school?"

I sighed. *She* would understand.

"Oh!" she said doubtfully. There was another long silence. Not knowing what else to do, I made a great show of studying my book.

"What are you reading, young man, so serious young man?" she smiled.

I turned the book around.

Surprise and delight showed in her face. "You study

French? You already perhaps speak it? I call it my other
language! From the time I was a girl in Odessa I study
it with application and pleasure. How pleasing to speak
French with you as I wait for your mother! We can con-
verse?"

"Yes, Mrs. Solovey," I fumbled. *"Il . . . il me ferait?
Il me ferait très heureux."*

She laughed. *"Ferait? Pas du tout!* And you have not a
suggestion of the true ac-cent!" Then I heard her say to
me: "I suppose you are learning French only to read?
The way you do everything! But that is a mistake, I can
assure you! It is necessary to speak, to speak! Think how
you would be happy to speak French well! To speak a
foreign language is to depart from yourself. Do you not
think it is tiresome to speak the same language all the time?
Their language! To feel that you are in a kind of prison,
where the words you speak every day are like the walls
of your cell? To know with every word that you are the
same, and no other, and that it is difficult to escape? But
when I speak French to you I have the sensation that for
a moment I have left, and I am happy."

I saw her timidly smiling at me. "Come, young man,
you will repeat your lesson to me?"

I read the exercise slowly from the book. *"Plus d'argent,
donc plus d'amusement. N'importe; j'aime mieux ne pas
m'amuser. Je n'ai dit mot à personne, et je n'en parlerai
pas de ma vie. Ni moi non plus."*

"Et vous?" she interrupted. *"Comment vous appelez-
vous?"*

"Alfred."

"Al-fred! *Voilà un joli nom! Un nom anglais, n'est-ce pas? En connaissez-vous l'origine?*"

"What?"

She sighed. "You know the origin of your name?"

"*Je pense . . . pense . . . un roi d'Angleterre?*"

"*Bien sûr. Et la légende des petits gâteaux?*"

"What?"

She tried again, very slowly.

I shook my head.

"But what is it they teach you in this American public school!"

"We're not up to irregular verbs."

"The old peasant woman, she asked the king to watch the cakes on the hearth. That they should not burn. But he thought and thought only of his poor country as he sat there, and he let them burn."

"*La vieille paysanne . . . était . . . était . . .*"

"*Fâchée! Ex-cel-lent!* She was very, very displeased. *Que c'est facile!* You must not stop now. Tell me something about yourself. *Quel âge avez-vous?*"

"*Quinze.*"

"*Vous avez quinze ans.* My older girl, she is only nine. *Maintenant, dites-moi: qu'est-ce que vous aimez le mieux au monde?*"

"*J'aime . . . j'aime . . .*"

"You have not understood me at all! I must be more careful to speak slowly. *Quand-je-parle-comme-ceci-me-comprenez-vous?*"

"*Oui.*"

"*Bien. Qu'est-ce que vous aimez le mieux au monde?*"

"*Livres.*"

"*Les livres!*" She laughed. "*Quel genre de livres?*"

"*Roman.*"

"*Le roman?*"

"*Poésie.*"

"*La poésie!*"

"*L'histoire. Les voyages.*"

"*Tout ça? Tout? Vous êtes un peu pédant.*"

"What?"

She sighed. "Does your mother come back very soon?"

"Soon! Soon!"

"Let us try again. What is it not books you like? *La mer?*"

"*Oui. J'aime la mer beaucoup.*"

"*J'aime beaucoup la mer. Encore.*"

"*J'aime beaucoup la mer.*"

"*Et puis?*"

"*Les montagnes.*"

"*Et ensuite?*"

"I know what I want to say, but don't know how to say it."

"*Le cinéma? Le sport? Les jeunes filles? Les jeunes filles ne vous déplaisent pas, naturellement?*"

"Yes," I said. "I like some girls very much. But . . . it's on the tip of my tongue . . ."

"*Pas en anglais!*"

"Well," I said, "I like summer."

"Summer! And the other seasons?"

"*Le printemps, l'automne, l'hiver?*"

"*Combien font trois fois trois?*"

"*Neuf.*"

"*Combien font quarante et vingt-six?*"

"*Soixante-six.*"

"*Pourquoi préférez-vous l'été?*"

"*La . . . la chaud?*" I gave it up. "The warmth . . . the evenness."

She stared at me silently, in gratitude. I distinctly heard her say: "I understand very well. I feel sympathy with your answer! I myself come from Odessa in the south of Russia. You know of Odessa? On the Black Sea. One of the most beautiful cities in all the world, full of sun. It is really a part of Greece. When I was a girl in Odessa, I would go down to the harbor every day and stare out across the water and imagine myself on a ship, a ship with blue sails, that would take me around the world."

"You have lived in many places."

"*Oui. Nous avons habité des pays différents. La Russie, la France, l'Italie, la Palestine.* Yes, many places."

"Why did you come *here?*" I asked suddenly.

She looked at me for a moment. I could not tell what she felt, or how much I had betrayed. But in some way my question wearied her. She rose, made a strange stiff little bow, and went out.

Occasionally I saw her in the street. She made no effort to continue my practice in French, and I did not know how to ask. For a long time I did not see her at all. We knew that Mr. Solovey had gone bankrupt, and was looking for someone to buy the fixtures. There were rumors on the block that once, in the middle of the night, he had beaten her so violently that people in the other tenement had been awakened by her screams. But there was nothing definite we knew about them, and after many weeks in which I vainly looked for her everywhere and

once tried to get into their apartment from the yard, I
almost forgot her. The store was finally sold, and Mr.
Solovey became an assistant in a drugstore on Blake Avenue. They continued to live in the apartment on the
ground floor. One morning, while her children were at
school, and her husband was at work, Mrs. Solovey sealed
all the doors and windows with adhesive tape, and sat
over the open gas jets in the kitchen until she was dead.
It was raining the day they buried her. Because she was
a suicide, the rabbi was reluctant to say the necessary
prayers inside the synagogue. But they prevailed upon
him to come out on the porch, and looking down on the
hearse as it waited in the street, he intoned the service
over her coffin. It was wrapped in the blue and white
flag with a Star of David at the head. There were hun-
dreds of women in their shawls, weeping in the rain. Most
of them had never seen Mrs. Solovey, but they came to
weep out of pity for her children, and out of terror and
awe because someone was dead. My mother was in the
front line outside the synagogue, and I needed urgently
to see her. But the crowd was so large that I could not
find her, and I waited in the back until the service was
over.

SUMMER: THE WAY

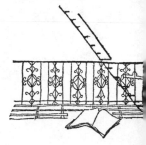

TO HIGHLAND PARK

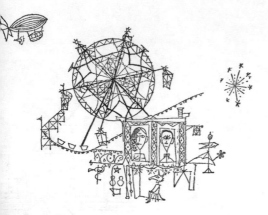

SUMMER was the passage through. I remember first the long stone path next to a meadow in Prospect Park where as a child I ran off one summer twilight just in time to see the lamplighter go from lamp to lamp touching each gas mantle with the upraised end of a pole so that it suddenly flamed. On the other side of those lamps, the long meadow was stormy-green and dark; but along the path, the flames at each lamp flared in yellow and green petals. Then, that summer I first strayed off the block for myself, the stone steps leading up from the lake in Prospect Park had stalks of grass wound between their cracks, were white with dust and drops of salt I thought came from the peanuts whose smell was everywhere in the park. But there was also some sugary taste in the air that day like the glazed wrapper around the cracker-jack box—and at the bottom of the box, caught by my sticky fingers, some fife or whistle which I blew that glorious warm Sunday full of cars from all over and the Stars and Stripes over the bandstand and the band in their colored coats and the dust flying up from every-body's shoes as we came over to hear.

Summer was the great time. I think now with a special joy of those long afternoons of mildew and quietness in the school courtyard, now a lazy playground, and of the cool stored-up basketball sweat along the silence of the main hall, where the dust rose up brown as we played quoits against the principal's door. Then of those holi-days even on weekdays when my mother would cry out as she suddenly wiped the sweat off her neck, "Oh, how hot it is today! *Too* hot! *Too* hot!" and decide on a day at Coney Island.

It was this pause that gave me my first idea of summer: life could slow down. Walking with my mother to the El at the other end of Sutter Avenue, I would stop under the awning of the remnants store to watch the light fall-ing through the holes in the buttons lining the window, and as we went past Belmont Avenue would stare in hungry pleasure at the fruits and vegetables on the open stands, the cherries glistening with damp as the storekeeper walked under his awning lightly passing a watering can over them; I would smell the sweat on the horses pulling the Italians' watermelon wagons—"Hey you ladies! *Freschi and good!*"; and breathe in the cloying sweetness of the caramels and chocolate syrup in the candy wholesaler's, the fumes of Turkish cigarettes from the "Odessa" and "Roumanian" tearooms, the strange sweetness from the splintered discarded crates where blotches of rotted fruit could still be seen crushed against the nailheads.

It was from the El on its way to Coney Island that I caught my first full breath of the city in the open air. Groaning its way past a thousand old Brooklyn red fronts and tranquil awnings, that old train could never go slowly enough for me as I stood on the open platform between the cars, holding on to the gate. In the dead calm of noon, heat mists drifted around the rusty green spires of unknown churches; below, people seemed to kick their heels in the air just a moment before being swept from my sight. With each homey crásh-crásh crásh-crásh of the wheels against the rails, there would steal up at me along the bounding slopes of the awnings the nearness of all those streets in middle Brooklyn named after generals of the Revolutionary War. I tasted the sweetness of summer on every opening in my face. As we came back at night along the El again, the great reward of the long parched day, far better than any massed and arid beach, was the chance to stand up there between the cars, looking down on the quiet streets unrolling below me as we passed. The rusty iron cars ground against each other, protesting they might fall apart at each sharp turn. But in the steady crásh-crásh crásh-crásh there was a comforting homeward sound as the black cars rocked on the rails and more and more men and boys in open shirts came out on the platform fiercely breathing the wind-charged damp air. In the summer night the city had an easy unstitched look—people sat on the corner watching the flies buzz around the street lamps, or at bedroom windows openly yawning as they stared past us.

Then home again, to the wet newsprint smell of the first editions of the *News* on the stands and the crackle of the hot dogs in the delicatessen windows—back to the old folks sitting outside our tenement on kitchen chairs, biting into polly seeds and drinking ice water out of milk bottles. Red and blue lights wink untiringly at us from the movie's long electric sign at the other end of Chester Street; the candy stores and delicatessens are ablaze. In the sky a blimp like a feebly smoking cigar floats in from some naval base along the coast. The dampness of the summer evening is in the last odors of all the suppers on the block, the salt in the air, the voices storming at each other behind the yellow window shades, the cries of the boys racing each other around the block. In a moment of unbelievable quiet a girl across the way can be heard stickily trying note on note from *Für Elise* on an untuned box piano. The tones buzz against my grateful brain, gather themselves up into one swelling wave before they fall into the theme, then resume like a fly complaining its way up a windowpane. Silhouetted against the window shade in the hard burning whiteness of her kitchen, young Mrs. C., who does not know anyone is watching, stands stripped to the waist at the kitchen sink,

washing herself down with yellow soap. Her long black
hair trails down her back, and her breasts swell in the
light, revealing the life hidden in their nakedness, soft as
the heart of a fruit. On the rooftop over the hardware
store the boys spring the pigeons from their cages, and
against the wisps of smoke in the air colored by the movie
sign the pigeons now begin their evening course—racing
each other furiously in bobbing circles above their own
roof, then widening and widening their flight from our
roof to the water tank to the movie sign. Two blocks
away, where the Italians begin at the other end of Rockaway Avenue, there is an aged sycamore with withered
leaves. The pigeons go round this tree at every other
flight, floating up and down as they urge their wings
against the air. The flights now grow narrower and narrower each time the pigeons pass our roof; at the last round
they alight quietly next to their own cages again, their
wings flapping breathlessly against their sides, some diffident
hoarse cry muffled in their throats as they are pressed back
into their cages.

Across the way a girl lies in bed, lazily scratching her
legs as she reads the comics in the *News*. Her young
brothers have been bedded in for the night on the fire
escape, and wedged between the ladder and the railing,
they now crouch in on themselves, their heads bent and
their knees up to the chin, like children still in the womb.
All along the block children are sleeping on the fire escapes. It is as hot tonight as it was this morning: first
scorched, then damp. The thickness of the summer night
weighs on us like wet wool. It is hard to breathe, to
move. The old folks sit on their kitchen chairs in weary

silence, cooling themselves with palmetto fans. The children on the fire escape giggle to each other as Negroes pass down the block on their way back to Livonia Avenue, singing aloud. One boy makes a feint at another, in playful attack. Suddenly a scream bursts out of the street: "Are you crazy? You'll fall to your death! Go to sleep or you'll be put back in the house!" It is near midnight, but no one can bear to go to bed. The rooms smell like burning sulphur. The heat stored up inside all through the day now oozes from the walls and blows its gritty breath on the faces of the sleepless people along the pavement. Hour by hour, the mounds of discarded polly seeds at each chair grow higher. The street is smeared with the blotched edges of ice-cream cones; every time I run around the block, the pavement clinks with empty coke bottles. By one o'clock whole families have gone to bed together on the roof, but the older boys sit on the edge, their feet dangling in the air. On the fire escapes the children hug each other for safety as they feel themselves falling asleep.

Summer nights meant street meetings. One night there was even a sudden visitation of Negro Jews from Harlem, who came to Brownsville seeking us out. They raised their platform on our corner, and a gnarled, very tall old man with a long bony face stood on it for hours delivering a passionate address on the ties uniting all children of Israel. I remember how the cheekbones worked in his face and how the gray little Assyrian beard leaped into the air as he threw his arms out in entreaty. The crisp

"American" eloquence of his speech bewildered me as I listened to him from the open window of that room, now mine, where our cousin had lived with us for so many years. Not a person on the block walked up to hear him; the old people sat cautiously in their usual places in front of the tenements, staring at him with wonder and suspicion, as if he were a barker calling them to enter his tent. Negroes were the *shvartse,* the blacks. We just did not think about them. They were people three and four blocks away you passed coming home from the subway. I never heard a word about them until the depression, when some of the younger ones began to do private painting jobs below the union wage scales, and when still another block of the earliest wooden shacks on Livonia Avenue near the subway's power station filled up with Negroes. Then some strange, embarrassed resentment would come out in the talk around the supper table. They were moving nearer and nearer. They were invading our neighborhood.

But summer evenings that second year of the depression, when you went up Pitkin Avenue in the usual Friday evening procession to the corner of the savings bank, the young Communists seemed to talk only of *our oppressed Negro brothers* and of the *Black Belt* for Negroes alone they wanted to see in the South. The very way you pronounced *Negro* was a test of your political maturity. Communists came out with the word respectfully and warmly, and with a certain plain indignation held in readiness against those who might even think of saying anything else. The little band of young Socialists with whom I met Sunday evenings in the Labor Lyceum on

Powell Street could never seem to say *Negro* with any
particular emotion. And as the young Communists said
sneeringly to us whenever they came around to break up
a meeting and to argue us into joining them, we had no
Negro comrades of our own.

Sitting on the steps of the Labor Lyceum in that loneliest of all Sunday evenings that came after a Socialist
meeting, I could still see high above the chill and dusty
tile floors in the entrance the enormous head and thick
beard of Karl Marx. The black ribbon of his spectacles
lay across a frock coat that seemed to bulge with defiance, and his lapels still shone smooth in the old photograph under glass. Next to him a picture of our dear
Gene Debs—his bald head glittering in the light of a single
bulb hung over the hallway, his mouth fixed in a shy
smile that made me ache to its distant goodness. *"While
there is a lower class I am of it, while there is a criminal
class I am of it, while there is a soul in prison I am not
free."* "Poor Parnell!" I would say under my breath. "My
dead King!" Inside the Labor Lyceum there had been
even on the hottest summer night that peculiarly stale chill
up and down the hallway where I could see the dirt
black between the tiles and read *A Portrait of the Artist
as a Young Man* to the creak of the folding chairs as the
meeting droned on to the report of the educational di-
rector. But there on the steps, listening to the Communist
hecklers through the ringing of the pinball machine and
the malted milk frothing in the candy store next door, I
pined for those long stale rooms where I had been safe
and asleep with my own. Socialists were not deep; they
laughed if you read too much; but they were wistful

and good-humored and lazy; they told Yiddish jokes in the meeting; I had been of them all my life. They were one big Brownsville family that lived on nostalgic anec- dotes of the great days before the Tammany Irishers had gerrymandered the district, when Brownsville had sent Socialists to the State Assembly and the Board of Alder- men. The local leaders were our benevolent uncles who had made good in the outside world as lawyers and dentists and teachers but would always stand up with us,

> *No more tradition's chains shall bind us!*
> *Arise ye slaves! No more in thrall!*

to press us toward what Norman Thomas, with that clean hearty "American" ring to his voice, always called on such an earnest downsweep of his right arm *the common- wealth of hand and brain.*

But the Communists who came after us Sunday eve- nings in the Labor Lyceum were not cozy at all. They were all somehow a little like Mendy, who was to go straight from Brownsville to Spain—tightly rolled together of sureness and contempt. I remember how the cold white tip of his nose shone in the light from the candy store next door, and how that cowlick that always seemed mys- teriously to threaten *me* frothed over his eyes as, pa- tronizing, icy and detached, he denounced the German Socialists who in 1914 had voted for the war credits, the English Socialists who in 1926 had sold out the General Strike, the Socialists everywhere who that summer of 1931 were selling out England, Germany, and Milwaukee, Wisconsin.

The keyword was always *sellout.* History had prepared

us to expect great things of the future, but something
or someone was always selling us out. "Bevin! Noske!
Scheidemann! Hillquit! Sellout after sellout after sellout!" *Sellouts* alone made it possible for us to talk together.
What else would the Communist voice on the bank corner have talked about—the callousness of Herbert Hoover?
the evictions that now took place on our block every day?
the stupidity of the Tammany District leader, that "good
Jew" who was Brooklyn's Commissioner of Records and
could not read or write? You were a worker or a worker's son; you were poor; you were a Jew—it was more
than enough. That voice on the bank corner knew our
complaints through and through, wrapped itself around
the elemental assent of each body in that crowd. No one
really listened. There was life only at the back of the
crowd, where it dribbled out into unwearied debates between individual Communists and Socialists. Sometimes
the pressure of those arguments would reach around the
speaker's stand, push it over, fill up the evening with the
unquenchable bitterness between worker and worker.
And then the real point of the evening would begin for
me as I went round from circle to circle listening to the
arguments. Long after midnight you could still see them
up and down Pitkin Avenue—two inflamed faces holding
the center, a great crowd around them adding to and
tensely sharing in each new point made about Germany
in 1914, Germany in 1919, England in 1926, Milwaukee
in 1931.

The way anywhere those summer evenings led through
the rival meetings on Pitkin Avenue. I could always find
people there. Socialism would come to banish my lone-

liness. Night after night now, going up Chester to Pitkin, I could not wait to get to the end of the street. The old beat-up boards of the synagogue porch looked frayed in the light, and the *shammes* sat on the steps desolately picking his nose as he frowned over the kids playing a last game of boxball in the gutter. From below the long glittering electric sign STADIUM   ALWAYS A GOOD PICTURE AT THE STADIUM   STADIUM the thick sweet fumes of deodorant out of the gents' were now stale and uninviting. Pitkin Avenue was already ablaze. From blocks away you could hear the Communist voice on the bank corner shouting into the great dark crowd, and some wistful Socialist voice on the opposite corner crying in rebuttal, and before you knew where you were, a sea of faces from Woolworth's to Kresge's had lifted you on its strong angry tide and had flung you against the gray marble wall of the savings bank. "WORKERS AND PEOPLE OF BROWNSVILLE . . . ! HOW LONG WILL YOU . . . !"

Sometimes we would walk up Pitkin Avenue with them after both meetings had collapsed under the storm of private arguments, ourselves still bitterly arguing each inch of the way. On the nights the Communists held "open meetings" in their headquarters on Thatford Avenue, they would lead us up endless staircases to a huge loft where the walls seemed to crackle with their tension and were lined round and round with long canvas red-painted strips crying DEFEND THE SOVIET UNION and FREE TOM MOONEY and THE SOCIALIST PARTY IS THE THIRD PARTY OF CAPITALISM. And often, after one of those regular Friday evening battles on Pitkin Avenue, I would meet up with them again on the benches in Betsy Head

Park, where one night the local C.P. organizer told me that I could not join even if I wanted to, for I was a student, not a *worker,* and as we sat arguing France, Italy, Germany, and the British General Strike of 1926, I could hear the spiked shoes of a boy in the darkness below running round and round the track.

It was to the sound of *The Waste Land* being read aloud that I met David. Whenever I got tired of flopping around the dusty streets and rang Isrolik's bell, the banister smelled of damp, the mother sat on a kitchen chair moaning against her unemployed husband as she stared at the sink, and from the city relief checks and cold family despair in that house Isrolik would start up with his glassy imperturbable poet's smile: "What an idiot! You still walking around in this heat? Come in and listen to Eliot! Everybody else is here!"

They lived on the ground floor, in a perpetual sour smell from the backyard. Wherever you sat in that house, you saw the clotheslines in the yard. On the round table in the "dining room," Isrolik's study by day and a bedroom for the four younger children at night, lay the hallowed copy of *The Waste Land* that he carried around with him wherever he went, and his regular offering of *Poetry, The New Masses,* squares of chocolate *Halvah,* biscuit sandwiches filled with a soft vanilla cream beginning to run in the heat, and bottles of seltzer. Isrolik and I never took to each other, but he was the first boy I knew in Brownsville who cared for poetry, and who even wrote it. So despite all my uneasiness in his house, it al-

ways astonished and excited me to sit around that table
with him and David and two or three other boys who
would listen gravely, munching the biscuit sandwiches
and drinking seltzer as Isrolik read aloud from *The Waste
Land*, and then comment on the *technic* and the *symbolism*.

I had never seen such boys before; I had not known
they existed in Brownsville. There was one they privately
called the *hunchback*, for his head was so enormous that
it looked ready to fall of its own weight back on his
spine. He was so ashamed that he never looked anyone
in the face, and from time to time would mumble quota-
tions he hoped someone would recognize and so begin to
talk with him. Whenever we all went about in the evenings—to the Free Theater on East 27th Street to see
Rosmersholm or *Ghosts*, to the Civic Repertory to see
Eva Le Gallienne in *Hedda Gabler*, to Lincoln Terrace
Park to pick up a girl—he walked behind us whispering
lines from *The Ballad of Reading Gaol* to see if we knew
the next ones. There was another, his cheeks so pitted with
acne that it was as if muddy wheels had passed over his
face, who spoke every word with an Oxford accent. Whenever you sat next to him, you could hear each sharp in-
take of his breath like a hiss. There was still another, with
a small growth of beard—they called him Ilyich, in honor
of Lenin—a boy much older than the rest of us, a strange
boy who lived by himself in a furnished room off Dumont Avenue, who had sworn never to shave until the
boss class freed Tom Mooney. His long matted hair and
beard gave him so archaic a look that I could never take
it in that he was really there with me, talking in his gently
condescending voice as I stared at the clotheslines. He

seemed to be someone I had remembered from a book, or perhaps even from a dream, about Russian intellectuals sitting around a hut in Siberia early in the century.

It was his feeling for poetry that held me to Isrolik's damp cluttered "study" those summer evenings. Wherever I looked, there were loose sheets of his own poems on the table, the floor, the beds, thrown in with stray issues of *Poetry*, commentaries on Eliot, and poems torn out of *The New Masses*. If Isrolik had to go into the kitchen to quiet his mother down, or to feed one of the children, or had to speak to us about anything not directly connected with poetry, he became irritable and impatient, tapped his feet and giggled nervously in his high thin voice until he could get back to reading from *The Waste Land*, a poem he loved with such breathless adoration that I seemed to see him sucking on each phrase like a lozenge he could not bear to swallow. Even when we tried to make money selling Eskimo Pies on the Coney Island beach, he would cry SHANTIH SHANTIH SHANTIH as we thrashed our way through the sands.

Yet in some way that puzzled me—I was so grateful to him for living two blocks away—I felt uneasy in his presence, and whenever I listened to him reading from *The Waste Land* to the sound of the mother moaning in the kitchen, I kept expecting a scream, a blow, perhaps even a fire, to bring things to a head in that house. How grim, sour and alone I felt as we walked around Brownsville those summer evenings arguing Keats and Shelley, Blake and Coleridge, Trotsky and Stalin. It was the second summer of the depression: my father had not worked for nine months, and every Friday evening as we sat down to eat my mother cried out: "Better I should work all night than we should take from the city!" Spain had a republic at last, and in England Ramsay MacDonald had just stabbed the Labor Party to the heart. I remember how we stopped in a school playground off Powell Street to play one last furious game of handball in the fading light; how, in front of a cutlery store on Belmont Avenue whose windows were ablaze with light, I stood looking at all those scissors and knives as Isrolik and his friends cried "Sellouts! Sellouts!" along my right ear. I felt that loneliness that shamed me after Socialist meetings on the steps of the Labor Lyceum—a loneliness I felt even in the massed and steaming "adults'" library on Glenmore Avenue, where all the future young lawyers sat at their law books with green eye-shades fixed over their faces like a second frown of attention; and in Lincoln Terrace Park, where old men played chess in the light from the street lamps. As we sat around all night arguing France, Germany, China, Italy, Spain, I hungrily listened to the girls squealing in the grass below.

The best of that bunch was David. He was a chemist, but I understood him better than I did Isrolik. David loved Beethoven, and *The Marriage of Heaven and Hell*; he could always predict in advance the days on which Macy's would put Modern Library books up for thirty-eight cents; and though entirely devoted to chemistry and the *Negro question* and forever blinking at me uneasily from behind his thick glaring lenses, he would sit in our "dining room" every late Friday afternoon reading aloud in a clear voice the essays and poems and sketches I had written at the kitchen table that week, and from time to time say with a heartwarming smile: "That's good! That's a pretty good phrase! I really think you're improving!" Crowded summer nights in the "adults'" library on Glenmore Avenue, how good it was to run into David in the fiction section—just there, where Gogol's *Summer Evenings on a Farm Near Dikánka* seemed to me the most beautiful title I had ever seen—how good just to walk him home to East New York, singing themes from the Beethoven Violin Concerto as we went.

It was poorer at his end than where we lived; most of the houses were the oldest tenements, with wooden staircases; when you went up the street bridge that led past the railroad yards, the streets looked as if they had cracked under the hot steam and the thunder from the freight cars being shuttled below. Along the route there were old tinsmith shops in basements, little unpainted wooden synagogues so old and bent and squeezed for space that you could see the boards loose in the walls; sweatshops where they made artificial flowers and ladies' slips until late in the evening. But I preferred it there; the nearer I got to David's house, the deeper I seemed to enter into Brownsville's frankness. Here was the other border, as far as possible from the *alrightniks* on Eastern Parkway; here was the turn-off for Highland Park, the transfer point to all good things that summer I was sixteen. The minute I went up the cracked and moldy wooden steps of David's house, my heart began to race against the thunder from the railroad yards. "Go over! Go over!"

The thing I always saw first in David's dining room was the far wall solidly covered with newspaper pictures of lynchings, pickets being beaten up by the police,

Ukrainian wheat fields from *Soviet Russia Today*, photographs, torn out of books, of Lenin, Toussaint L'Ouverture, Frederick W. Douglass, Henri Barbusse, and Ernst Thaelmann. On the bureau next to his chemistry texts, ranged in front of the glass so that you saw their backs reflected in the glass whenever you looked at them, were the collected works of Lenin. On the wall above hung the usual oval photographs of the grandfather and grandmother, side by side staring down at me where I had nervously caught my shoes in the holes of the dark-brown linoleum. Whenever I looked away from those pictures on the far wall of Negroes hanging from the boughs of trees in the deep South, I would see those dead grandparents gloomily taking me in, and would feel that I had come up too close to some strange stone carving in the desert and had fallen between the cracks.

On those hot summer evenings you could hear through the screens the endless charging of the freight cars in the yards. The mother, already yellow with cancer, sat silently and stiffly propped up on pillows; a young boy sat at her feet waving a palmetto fan, and whenever she cried out, would glare up at me fiercely and dash into the kitchen for another glass of water. In that house the light of the early summer evening had the same yellowness as the mother's face. She was small, with her hair oddly cut short like a boy's; and whenever I saw her, wore an old patched middy blouse; the yellowness of that room ran in sick querulous waves down into the bandages thick over her left breast. From the stale weedy garden patch in the old "private" house next door, the dusty prong of an old tree pressed against the window screen, and when the screen rattled in the sudden windy darkening of the air before a rainstorm, seemed to expel a thin layer of dust into the room.

Everything in that house looked as if it had come down to a few minimum utensils for eating, sleeping, and dying. I remember the peculiar desolation of the broken dining room chairs around the table, and how, every time I moved, my shoes seemed to catch in the holes of the linoleum. Yet far more than the poverty in that orphaned and rotting house; more, even, than the sense of impending death, it was some deep, brave, and awful earnestness before life itself I always felt there. From time to time I would even catch in the air the curious, unbelievable idea that David had stripped their life deliberately to those chemistry textbooks, the collected works of Lenin, those Negroes on the far wall hanged, castrated, and burned in darkest Georgia. I had never seen such a naked house. And that it should be lived in so indifferently; that David should walk so carelessly across the hollows in the linoleum as he went over to the bureau to seize a fresh volume of Lenin that might purge me of my *confusions* and harden me up at last; that the mother herself, whether from interest or despair, should ignore everything there but our bitter arguments as she silently looked down at us—it was just this that kept me coming back. The house was so naked, everyone in it seemed entirely free to think.

It was the lapping of the water against the wire fence I heard most below the sound of my voice when we went

round and round the old reservoir. Those still, perfectly
hot afternoons, Highland Park was so quiet, you could
hear children talking to each other in the empty bandstand below, the drip of the water fountains down in
the park, a girl laughing at the other end of the path
around the reservoir. The reservoir rose at the very top
of a hill; the hill overlooked the last of Brooklyn, the
thousands of tombstones in the great cemeteries just beyond, distant windows blinking in the skyscrapers white
in the sun over midtown Manhattan. But no one ever
seemed to go to Highland Park much; the reservoir itself,
they said, had not been used for years. Even in the middle
of a June afternoon, the graveled path around it was so
quiet, I could hear the water lapping against the wire fence.

We used to go round and round it, reading in turns
all I had suddenly begun to write that year. It was the
summer of my graduation from high school, the beginning of that cardinal summer at sixteen when, day after
day, wild with gratitude and surprise, I began to take in
what I would live for. He must have been a very young
man then, not long out of the city college to which I in
my turn would be going that fall; but very offhand,
forever drawling out sarcasms when he thought I
needed taking down, he seemed to me very settled and
wise in that thin, weary way he had; he never paid a
compliment to your face. Every warm full June afternoon that last week of high school, I would wait for him
on Evergreen Avenue, staring and staring at the trees
lining the quiet "American" streets beautiful with gray
frame houses and brownstones, and then we would walk
past the German ice-cream parlors and up Bushwick Ave-

nue in that extraordinary summer's peace under the awnings, stop at his house to hear Kreisler and Casals, and at last, steadily mounting the hill that led into Highland Park past Trommer's Brewery, go up to the reservoir through the cemetery, in which he once pointed out the place where a little group of Chinese lay all to themselves.

It always astonished me that he took so much trouble; he had never been a teacher of mine. But that last week, proctoring our final examination in Spanish, he had refused me permission to leave the room when I had turned in my papers before the closing bell, and when I had asked for something to read, he had flung me some more yellow test paper, and in his weary unamiable way, had said: "I suppose you can write? Write something!"

It had been about a violin. Walking along the street I had seen an old violin in a pawnshop window. It was snowing; people walked on every side of me, huddled against the storm; but I stood in front of that despised and neglected violin, remembering all the hands through which it had passed. I had shown it to him then and there, and he had read it with a grin; and still grinning, had taken me off to lunch; and that thin, weary, bitter grin more and more pronounced each day of that last week I ever saw him, he would lend me autobiographies by Russian Jews, picture books by Marc Chagall, and leading me off to Highland Park for a walk around the reservoir, make me read aloud from my notebook essays and poems and sketches.

Those June afternoons, it was the water lapping against the fence I kept listening for under the unexpected sound of my own voice. There was an old leftover rowboat, chained to the fence, that you could sometimes see the caretaker riding up and down in, dredging the old reservoir of its muck. I would listen for the boat restlessly beating at the fence, for the cries of children in the park, for anything that would take me away from the harsh exultant pain of hearing my own voice ring out on that quiet path.

Just below the path, raising their heads above the endless white crosses of a soldier's cemetery, were strange red flowers. I did not know their names. But when a sudden breeze scudded along the water, and on one long and single breath of wind the dust flew up from the graveled path and a castoff newspaper flew onto the webbed wire fence, those red flowers along the bottom of the hill would wave and shake and thrash on each other as if they were bleeding together, red pouring on red. From the path to those flowers just below, the way was a plunging fall. In the unbearable stillness of the almost empty park, once you had stopped reading, silence itself took over—a silence so keen, so heartbreakingly firm and implacable across the wide, endlessly wide surface of the water and the long even glare of the sun on the path, that it seemed to come out of the very middle of the air.

That summer I had my first regular job. Carrying a blue canvas bag in which I kept a book for private reading, I went about the streets of middle Brooklyn all through the long blazing afternoons picking up specimens from drugstores to be delivered to a urinalysis lab on Nostrand Avenue. Between drugstores on my route

I often stopped to read in various small parks along the
way. I remember how that faint distant odor curiously
reminiscent of stale ground-up peanuts clung to the blue
surface of the *David Copperfield* I was always reading on
the job, and that whenever I got lost in reading and rode
far past my destination, usually found that I had used up
the carfare the boss had given me and that I would have
to walk it the rest of the way. But then, in the brilliant
heat, the jars and flasks wrapped in brown paper bags
tinkling against each other as I walked, that faint odor
of stale ground-up peanuts lingering along the cracks in
the pavement, I gave myself to those streets I was lost
in as if I were swimming in the weather.

It was the intense silence and heat of those summer
streets that delivered me to all my joy. Whenever I
guiltily thrust *David Copperfield* back into my canvas
bag and started out fresh from some strange streetcar
crossing, I would rush off in a panic, thinking only of the
time I had lost and what the boss would say. Then the
silence of summer would fall on the top of my head,
cleaving me through and through, as if the front of my
face alone were rushing ahead to the next drugstore on
my list, while my spine dawdled in amazement. There
was suddenly anywhere to go now; I had the whole long
afternoon to walk around in. My summer's time had come;
my own time had come at last. There was a deep aromatic
coolness behind the awning of each new drugstore that
was made up of cleanness and camphor and the toilet
water seeping out of the vials on the counter, of the thick
black type and the priestly face on Father John's Cough
Medicine, of the clink of an empty spoon against the

smooth top of the soda fountain counter, of the dry fizz
of soda water backing out of the taps, of the stiff "American" dignity and starched linen jackets on all those strange
new Gentile druggists. The insides of all drugstores summer afternoons were hermetically deep. When I walked
into one under the awning, out of the glare, it was like
floating down to the bottom of a lake with my eyes wide
open among the rushes.

That particular great day in the heat, the unending
heat, I was walking somewhere off Gates Avenue, and
saw that they had unfurled awnings even over the El
stations. I could hear the plash of a fountain in a school
courtyard across the street; one whole side of that block
was lined with trees. How hot it was that afternoon. The
dust never stirred on the leaves of the nearest trees; the
pavements were so fierce that I kept walking under the
awnings of chain groceries to cool my breath and to sniff at
the fresh watered celery stalks on the open stands and the
clean, shaded interiors that smelled of coffee beans and
of biscuits. When I walked back into the sun, every mica
dot glittered in the pavement. From time to time, the hot
streets were racked by some dry, distant thunder from
the El. How hot it was that afternoon, how silent and hot.
As I started down that lonely stretch of sidewalk somewhere off Gates Avenue, everything moved so slowly
that I could almost count the drops of sweat bubbling
on a girl's upper lip, the sounds of my heart dreamily
pounding into my ears from the end of a long corridor
as she passed me, breasts rustling in her blouse, her blouse
gleaming in the sun like a second sheath of skin. All around
me the city seemed entirely at rest. There were so few

passers-by that I could feel the awnings over the shops pulling away from me in amazement and scorn, was queerer and more alone to myself than ever as I passed up that street with a trickle from some loosened jar seeping out of my bag.

And then it came. All the way down that street, there seemed to be nothing but myself with a bag, the blazingly hot and empty afternoon, and silence through which I pressed my way. But the large shadow on the pavement was me, the music in my head was me, the indescribable joy I felt was me. I was so happy, I could not tell what I felt apart from the evenness of the heat in which I walked. The sweat poured out of my body in relief. I was me, me, me, and it was summer.

Notice: Anyone placing any encumbrance on this balcony will be fined ten dollars. Now, when I sat on the fire escape evenings after work, the sky was the mirror of the book in my hand. I could have shown those open pages to the roofs and have read them back from the clouds moving over my head. From that private perch, everything in sight now loosed itself from its containing hard edges in space and came back to me as a single line of words burning across the page. Half-past five on a summer day—at my back I could smell soupgreens being put into the pot—just that hour which in the tense autumn of school beginning again or in the blindness of winter at the bottom of the year is so dark, but which now brims over with light you can breathe and breathe in with the iron grit flaking off the sign on the fire escape: Notice:

ANYONE PLACING ANY ENCUMBRANCE ON THIS BALCONY
WILL BE FINED TEN DOLLARS.

Look how much light there is. It does not matter now
that your bottom itches to the pebbly stone on the windowsill; that the sun is so fierce, it burns your feet on
the iron planks; that when you get up to stretch your
legs, the heat makes you so dizzy, you can see yourself
falling down the red-painted ladders that chase each other
to the street. For now a single line of English words
takes you up slowly, and slowly carries you across the
page to where, each time you reach its end, you have to
catch your breath and look away—the pleasure is unbearable, it is so full.

But when that which is perfect is *come, then that which
is in part* shall *be done away.*

When I was *a child, I spake as a child, I understood as
a child, I thought as a child; but when I became a man, I
put away childish things.*

*For now we see through a glass, darkly; but then face
to face: now I know in part; but then shall I know* even
as also I am known.

The man from whom I had accepted the little blue
volume on the Fifth Avenue steps of the Library had
said to me in Yiddish, searching my face doubtfully:
"You *are* a Jew? You will really look into it?" No, I was
not really looking into it; I could not read more than two
or three pages at a time without turning away in excitement and shame. Would the old women across the street
ever have believed it? But how square and hardy the

words looked in their even black type. Each seemed to burn separately in the sun as I nervously flipped the pages and then turned back to where the book most naturally lay flat: *For now we see through a glass, darkly*. Each time my eye fell on that square even black type, the sentence began to move in the sun. It rose up, a smoking frame of dark glass above the highest roofs, steadily and joyfully burning, as, reading aloud to myself, I tasted the rightness of each word on my tongue.

It was like heaping my own arms with gifts. There were images I did not understand, but which fell on my mind with such slow opening grandeur that once I distinctly heard the clean and fundamental cracking of trees. First the image, then the thing; first the word in its taste and smell and touch, then the thing it meant, when you were calm enough to look. Images were instantaneous; the meaning alone could be like the unyielding metal taste when you bit on an empty spoon. The initial shock of that language left no room in my head for anything else. But now, each day I turned back to that little blue testament, I had that same sense of instant connectedness I had already noticed in myself to the exclamation *O altitudo!* in a quotation from Sir Thomas Browne; to the chapter on the cathedral in Lawrence's *The Rainbow;* to the opening line of Henry Vaughan's "The World,"

I saw Eternity the other night

that haunted me from the day I came on it in an anthology; to Blake's

> *When the stars threw down their spears*
> *And water'd heaven with their tears,*
> *Did he smile his work to see?*
> *Did he who made the Lamb make thee?;*

to the opening lines of *A Farewell to Arms,* indescribably dry and beautiful with the light on those pebbles in the plain; to *When Lilacs Last in the Dooryard Bloom'd,* where I knew as soon as I came on the line

> *Passing the yellow-spear'd wheat, every grain*
> *from its shroud in the dark brown fields uprisen.*

that I had found another writer I could instinctively trust.

First the image, then the sense. First those clouds moving blue and white across the nearest roofs; and then—*O altitudo!,* the journey into that other land of *flax,* of summer, eternal summer, through which *he* had walked, wrapped in a blue and white prayer shawl, and, still looking back at me with the heartbreaking smile of recognition from a fellow Jew, had said: *The blind receive their sight, and the lame walk, the lepers are cleansed, and the deaf hear, the dead are raised up, and the poor have the gospel preached to them.*

And blessed is he, whosoever shall not be offended in me.

Offended in him? I had known him instantly. Surely I had been waiting for him all my life—our own Yeshua, misunderstood by his own, like me, but the very embodiment of everything I had waited so long to hear from a Jew—a great contempt for the minute daily business of

the world; a deep and joyful turning back into our own
spirit. It was *he*, I thought, who would resolve for me at
last the ambiguity and the long ache of being a Jew—
Yeshua, our own long-lost Jesus, speaking straight to the
mind and heart at once. For that voice, that exultantly
fiery and tender voice, there were no gaps between images
and things, for constantly walking before the Lord, he
remained all energy and mind, thrust his soul into every
corner of the world, and passing gaily under every yoke,
remained free to seek our God in His expected place.

How long I had been waiting for him, how long: like
metal for a magnet to raise it. I had recognized him immediately, and all over: that exaltation; those thorny
images that cut you with their overriding fervor and
gave you the husk of every word along with the kernel;
that furious old Jewish impatience with *Success*, with
comfort, with eating, with the rich, with the whole shabby
superficial fashionable world itself; that fatigue, as of a
man having constantly to make his way up and down the
world on foot; and then that sternness and love that
gushed out of him when he turned to the others and
said:

*For verily I say unto you, Till heaven and earth pass,
one jot or one tittle shall in no wise pass from the law,
till all be fulfilled.*

Yeshua my Yeshua! What had he to do with those
who killed his own and worshiped him as God? Why
would *they* call him only by that smooth Greek name of
Jesus? He was Yeshua, my own Reb Yeshua, of whose
terrible death I could never read without bursting into
tears—Yeshua, our own Yeshua, the most natural of us

all, the most direct, the most enchanted, and as he sprang up from the heart of poor Jews, all the dearer to me because he could now return to his own kind: *and the poor have the gospel preached to them.*

Ripeness filled our kitchen even at supper time. The room was so wild with light, it made me tremble; I could not believe my eyes. In the sink a great sandy pile of radishes, lettuces, tomatoes, cucumbers, and scallions broke up on their stark greens and reds the harshness of the world's daily monotony. The window shade by the sewing machine was drawn, its tab baking in the sun. Through the screen came the chant of the score being called up from the last handball game below. Our front door was open, to let in air; you could hear the boys on the roof scuffing their shoes against the gravel. Then, my father home to the smell of paint in the hall, we sat down to chopped cucumbers floating in the ice-cold borscht, radishes and tomatoes and lettuce in sour cream, a mound of corn just out of the pot steaming on the table, the butter slowly melting in a cracked blue soup plate—breathing hard against the heat, we sat down together at last.

Daylight at evening. The whitewashed walls have turned yellow in great golden combs, as if the butter dribbling down our chins from each new piece of corn we lovingly prepare with butter and salt were oozing down the walls. The kitchen is quiet under the fatigue blown in from the parched streets—so quiet that in this strangely drawn-out light, the sun hot on our backs, we seem to be eating hand in hand. "How hot it is still! How hot still!" The silence and calm press on me with a painful joy. I cannot wait to get out into the streets tonight, I cannot wait. Each unnatural moment of silence says that something is going on outside. Something is about to happen. The sound of an impending explosion waits in the summer night.

In the open, now. The sun hanging below the end of each block hits me in the face. They have opened the fire hydrants and have put up a revolving shower in the middle of the street, and kids stripped to their underwear run squealing in and out of the feebly sputtering drops. "*Mama! Look at me, Mama!*" Where the gutter is wet now, it glistens like rhinestones; where dry, it is blue. Halfway down the block a horse lies dead in the gutter, a cloud of flies buzzing at his eyes. A little carousel has drawn up next to the grocery. The hurdy-gurdy skips whole notes at a time, as if it were being pressed and squeezed out of shape each time the wooden horses with long straw manes come round again. The pony glumly relieves himself in his traces, and the sparrows float down from the telephone wires to peck and peck at each fresh steaming mound of manure, and the smell of the milk scum from the great open cans outside the grocery is suddenly joined, on a passing breath of wind, to the smell of varnish and brine from the barrels outside the warehouse on Bristol Street. Westward, on the streets that lead to the park, the dusty trees of heaven droop in the sun. You can smell Brownsville's tiredness in the air like smoke. Slowly, how slowly now, the pigeons rise and fall in their unchanging orbits as they go round and round the roofs, the enigmatic spire of the church, and brush against the aged sycamore with sharp leaves.

And now there is time. This light will not go out until I have lodged it in every crack and corner of me first.

There was a new public library I liked to walk out to right after supper, when the streets were still full of light. It was to the north of the Italians, just off the El on Broadway, in the "American" district of old frame houses and brownstones and German ice-cream parlors and quiet tree-lined streets where I went to high school. Everything about that library was good, for it was usually empty and cool behind its awnings, and the shelves were packed with books that not many people ever seemed to take away. But even better was the long walk out of Brownsville to reach it.

How wonderful it was in the still suspended evening light to go past the police station on East New York and come out into the clinging damp sweetness of Italian cheese. The way to the borders of Brownsville there was always heavy with blocks of indistinguishable furniture stores, monument works, wholesale hardware shops. Block after block was lined with bedroom sets, granite tombstones, kitchen ranges, refrigerators, store fixtures, cash registers. It was like taking one last good look around before you said good-by. As the sun bore down on new kitchen ranges and refrigerators, I seemed to hear the clang of all those heavily smooth surfaces against the fiery windows, to feel myself pulled down endless corridors of tombstones, cash registers, maple beds, maple love seats, maple vanity tables.

But at the police station, the green lamps on each side of the door, the detectives lounging along the street, the smell from the dark, damp, leaky steps that led down to the public toilets below, instantly proclaimed the end of Brownsville.

Ahead, the Italians' streets suddenly reared up into hills, all the trolley car lines flew apart into wild plunging crossroads—the way to anywhere, it seemed to me then. And in the steady heat, the different parts of me racing each other in excitement, the sweat already sweet on my face, still tasting on my lips the corn and salt and butter, I would dash over the tree-lined island at the crossroads, and on that boulevard so sharp with sun that I could never understand why the new red-brick walls of the Catholic church felt so cool as I passed, I crossed over into the Italian district.

I still had a certain suspicion of the Italians—surely they were all Fascists to a man? Every grocery window seemed to have a picture of Mussolini frowning under a feather-tipped helmet, every drugstore beneath the old-fashioned gold letters pasted on the window a colored lithograph of the Madonna with a luminescent heart showing through a blue gown. What I liked best in the windows were the thickly printed opera posters, topped by tiny photographs of singers with olive-bronze faces. Their long straight noses jutted aloofly, defying me to understand them. But despite the buzz of unfamiliar words ending in the letter *i*, I could at least make contact with LA FORZA DEL DESTINO. In the air was that high overriding damp sweetness of Italian cheese, then something peppery. In a butcher shop window at the corner of Pacific Street long incredibly thin sausage rings were strung around a horizontal bar. The clumps of red and brown meat dripping off those sausage rings always stayed with me until I left the Italians at Fulton Street—did they eat such things?

Usually, at that hour of the early evening when I passed through on my way to the new library, they were all still at supper. The streets were strangely empty except for an old man in a white cap who sat on the curb sucking at a twisted Italian cigar. I felt I was passing through a deserted town and knocking my head against each door to call the inhabitants out. It was a poor neighborhood, poor as ours. Yet all the houses and stores there, the very lettering of the signs Avvocato Farmacia Latteria tantalized me by their foreignness. Everything there looked smaller and sleepier than it did in Brownsville. There was a kind of mild, infinitely soothing smell of flour and cheese mildly rotting in the evening sun. You could almost taste the cheese in the sweat you licked off your lips, could feel your whole body licking and tasting at the damp inner quietness that came out of the stores. The heat seemed to melt down every hard corner in sight.

Beyond Atlantic Avenue the sun glared and glared on broken glass lining the high stone walls of a Catholic reformatory that went all around the block. Barbed wire rose up on the other side of the wall, and oddly serene above the broken glass, very tall trees. Behind those walls, I had always heard, lived "bad girls" under the supervision of nuns. We knew what all that broken glass meant. The girls stole out every night and were lifted over the walls every morning by their laughing boy friends. We knew. The place was a prison house of the dark and hypocritical

Catholic religion. Whenever I heard the great bell in the yard clanging for prayers as I passed, I had the same image in my mind of endless barren courts of narrow rooms, in each of which a girl in a prison smock looked up with pale hatred at a nun.

And priests in black gowns were walking their rounds
And binding with briars my joys and desires

Jesus! I would say to myself with hoped-for scorn, *Look at my Yeshua!* How I wanted to get on to my library, to get on beyond that high stone wall lined with the jagged ends of broken milk bottles; never to have to look back at that red-bricked church that reared itself up across from the borders of Brownsville like a fortress. Once, on the evening before an examination, I had gone into that church, had tried vaguely to pray, but had been so intimidated by the perpetual twilight, the remoteness of the freezing white altar and the Italian women in kerchiefs around me, that at a low murmuring out of a confession box near the door I had run away. Yet how lonely it always was passing under the wall—as if I were just about to be flung against it by a wave of my own thought.

Ahead of me now the black web of the Fulton Street El. On the other side of the BANCA COMMERCIALE, two long even pavements still raw with sunlight at seven o'clock of a summer evening take me straight through the German and Irish "American" neighborhoods. I could never decide whether it was all those brownstones and blue and gray frame houses or the sight of the library serenely waiting for me that made up the greatest pleasure of that early evening walk. As soon as I got out from under the darkness of the El on Fulton Street, I was catapulted into tranquillity.

Everything ahead of me now was of a different order—wide, clean, still, every block lined with trees. I sniffed hungrily at the patches of garden earth behind the black iron spikes and at the wooden shutters hot in the sun—there where even the names of the streets, Macdougal, Hull, Somers, made me humble with admiration. The long quiet avenues rustled comfortably in the sun; above the brownstone stoops all the yellow striped awnings were unfurled. Every image I had of peace, of quiet shaded streets in some old small-town America I had seen dreaming over the ads in the *Saturday Evening Post*, now came back to me as that proud procession of awnings along the brownstones. I can never remember *walking* those last few blocks to the library; I seemed to float along the canvas tops. Here were the truly American streets; here was where they lived. To get that near to brownstones, to see how private everything looked in that world of cool black painted floors and green walls where on each windowsill the first shoots of Dutch bulbs rose out of the pebbles like green and white flags, seemed to me the greatest privilege I had ever had. A breath of long-stored memory blew out at me from the veranda of Oyster Bay. Even when I visited an Irish girl from my high school class who lived in one of those brownstones, and was amazed to see that the rooms were as small as ours, that a Tammany court attendant's family could be as poor as we were, that behind the solid "American" front of fringed shawls,

Yankee rocking chairs, and oval daguerreotypes on the walls they kept warm in winter over an oil stove—even then, I could think of those brownstone streets only as my great entrance into America, a half-hour nearer to "New York."

I had made a discovery; I had stumbled on a connection between myself and the shape and color of time in the streets of New York. Though I knew that brownstones were old-fashioned and had read scornful references to them in novels, it was just the thick, solid way in which they gripped to themselves some texture of the city's past that now fascinated me. There was one brownstone on Macdougal Street I would stop and brood over for long periods every evening I went to the library for fresh books—waiting in front of it, studying every crease in the stone, every line in the square windows jutting out above the street, as if I were planning its portrait. I had made a discovery: walking could take me back into the America of the nineteenth century.

On those early summer evenings, the library was usually empty, and there was such ease at the long tables under the plants lining the windowsills, the same books of American history lay so undisturbed on the shelves, the wizened, faintly smiling little old lady who accepted my presence without questions or suggestions or reproach was so delightful as she quietly, smilingly stamped my card and took back a batch of new books every evening, that whenever I entered the library I would walk up and down trembling in front of the shelves. For each new book I took away, there seemed to be ten more of which I was depriving myself. Everything that summer I was

sixteen was of equal urgency—Renan's *Life of Jesus;* the
plays of Eugene O'Neill, which vaguely depressed me,
but were full of sex; Galsworthy's *The Forsyte Saga,* to
which I was so devoted that even on the day two years
later Hitler came to power I could not entirely take it in,
because on the same day John Galsworthy died; anything about Keats and Blake; about Beethoven; the plays
of W. Somerset Maugham, which I could not relate
to the author of *Of Human Bondage; The Educa-
tion of Henry Adams,* for its portrait of John Quincy
Adams leading his grandson to school; Lytton Strachey's
Eminent Victorians, for its portrait of Cardinal Newman,
the beautiful Newman who played the violin and was
seen weeping in the long sad evening of his life; Thomas
Mann's *Death in Venice,* which seemed to me vaguely
sinister and unbearably profound; Turgenev's *Fathers and
Sons,* which I took away one evening to finish on my fire
escape with such a depth of satisfaction that I could never
open the book again, for fear I would not recapture that
first sensation.

The automatic part of all my reading was history. The
past, the past was great: anything American, old, glazed,
touched with dusk at the end of the nineteenth century,
still smoldering with the fires lit by the industrial revolution, immediately set my mind dancing. The present was
mean, the eighteenth century too Anglo-Saxon, too far
away. Between them, in the light from the steerage ships
waiting to discharge my parents onto the final shore, was
the world of dusk, of rust, of iron, of gaslight, where, I
thought, I would find my way to that fork in the road
where all American lives cross. The past was deep, deep,

full of solitary Americans whose careers, though closed in death, had woven an arc around them which I could see in space and time—"lonely Americans," it was even the title of a book. I remember that the evening I opened Lewis Mumford's *The Brown Decades* I was so astonished to see a photograph of Brooklyn Bridge, I so instantly formed against that brownstone on Macdougal Street such close and loving images of Albert Pinkham Ryder, Charles Peirce, Emily Dickinson, Thomas Eakins, and John August Roebling, that I could never walk across Roebling's bridge, or pass the hotel on University Place named Albert, in Ryder's honor, or stop in front of the garbage cans at Fulton and Cranberry Streets in Brooklyn at the place where Whitman had himself printed *Leaves of Grass*, without thinking that I had at last opened the great trunk of forgotten time in New York in which I, too, I thought, would someday find the source of my unrest.

I felt then that I stood outside all that, that I would be alien forever, but that I could at least keep the trunk open by reading. And though I knew somewhere in myself that a Ryder, an Emily Dickinson, an Eakins, a Whitman, even that fierce-browed old German immigrant Roebling, with his flute and his metaphysics and his passionate love of suspension bridges, were alien, too, alien in the deepest way, like my beloved Blake, my Yeshua, my Beethoven, my Newman—nevertheless I still thought of myself then as standing outside America. I read as if books would fill my every gap, legitimize my strange quest for the American past, remedy my every flaw, let me in at last into the great world that was anything just out of Brownsville.

So that when, leaving the library for the best of all

walks, to Highland Park, I came out on Bushwick Avenue, with its strange, wide, sun-lit spell, a thankfulness seized me, mixed with envy and bitterness, and I waited against a hydrant for my violence to pass. Why were these people *here*, and we *there?* Why had I always to think of insider and outsider, of their belonging and our not belonging, when books had carried me this far, and when, as I could already see, it was myself that would carry me farther—beyond these petty distinctions I had so long made in loneliness?

But Highland Park was different; Highland Park was pure idea. To savor it fully at the end of a walk, I liked to start out fresh from Brownsville. Summer nights that year I was sixteen and she was fifteen, I used to meet her on East New York Avenue, at the corner of the police station. Our route was always up Liberty Avenue, where the old yellow frame houses looked like the remains of a mining town, and the cracks in the pavement opened a fissure that trailed into hills of broken automobile parts littering the junk shops.

The way to the park is north and west, past the Brooklyn line altogether. At the border, the trolley car lines and elevated lines snarl up into one last drab knot; then it is like a fist opening, and the way ahead is clear. We trudged up endless small city hills; except for the rattling of the freight cars in the railroad yards and an occasional watchman's light in the factories, the streets seemed entirely dead. We went past the factories, the freight yards, the hospital, the Long Island railroad station, an abandoned schoolhouse and an old pottery, its green roof

cracked and engraved in thousands of small lines, as if
everyone passing that way had knifed his name on it.
The way up the hills was always strange, no matter how
many times we followed it, for every step took us into the
parkway off Bushwick Avenue, with its latticed entrances
to the German beer gardens.

At Highland Boulevard the last of the factories van-
ished below the hill, and the park emerged in its summer
sweetness. At every corner along the boulevard there
were great trees; as we stopped at the top to catch our
breaths, the traffic lights turned red and green on the
trees and each leaf flushed separately in the colored light.
I used to watch the signals switching red and green on
the leaves. The click in the signal box had a humorous
sound on the deserted boulevard, and as the light poured
on the leaves, green and red, green and red, with a
moment's pause between them, I seemed to see some force
weary of custom, aroused against the monotony of day
and night, playing violently with color in the freedom of
the summer evening.

In those days the park lay open along the boulevard.
They were always making half-hearted repairs on it that
no one ever seemed to finish; we could enter the park anywhere—over the great stone fence above the cemetery;
or over planks the workmen had laid between mounds
of sand near the basketball court; or up its own hill to
the reservoir itself. It was somehow not a real park then,
not the usual city park—more like an untended wild
growth they had forgotten to trim to the shape of the
city. Most people I knew did not care for it; it was too
remote, and at night, almost completely dark. It ran past

interminable cemeteries where there seemed to be room for all the dead of New York.

But all this made the park more interesting to us. Our favorite way was past the mounds that stood just in from the boulevard. There was something in this I liked—a feeling that we were secretly descending on the park from a great height. I took her hand, and step by step, walking carefully over the planks the workmen had left, we went down into the empty park, past the basketball court, the gardens, the bandstand, until we could hear the old rowboat banging against the wire fence and climb up the hill to the reservoir.

From one side of the reservoir hill we could look across the cemetery to the skyscrapers of Manhattan; from the other, to miles of lampposts along Jamaica Avenue. Below us was a wood, then a military cemetery, slope on slope laid out in endless white crosses. We never tired of walking round the reservoir arm in arm, watching the light playing on the water, and going, as it seemed, from one flank of New York to the other. The city was no longer real; only a view from a distance, interrupted by cemeteries on every side. But on a summer night, when we lay in the grass below, the smell of the earth and the lights from the distant city made a single background to my desire. The lampposts winked steadily from Jamaica Avenue, and the YMCA's enormous sign glowed and died and glowed again. Somewhere in the deadness of the park the water gurgled in the fountains. In the warmth and stillness a yearning dry and sharp as salt rose in me. Far away a whistle hooted; far away girls went round and round the path, laughing. When we went home, taking the road past the cemetery, with the lights of Jamaica Avenue spread out before us, it was hard to think of them as something apart, they were searching out so many new things in me.